THE SPIRITED YEARS

THE SPIRITED YEARS

A HISTORY OF
THE ANTEBELLUM NAVAL ACADEMY

By Charles Todorich

NAVAL INSTITUTE PRESS
Annapolis, Maryland

Copyright © 1984
by the United States Naval Institute
Annapolis, Maryland

Library of Congress Cataloging in Publication Data
Todorich, Charles, 1948–
  The spirited years.

  Bibliography: p.
  Includes index.
  1. United States Naval Academy—History—19th century.
I. Title.
V415.LIT63   1984   359'.007'1173   83-27241
ISBN 0-87021-520-5

Printed in the United States of America

To Patty
for her patience and understanding
and to our children
Paige and Brent
for their inspiration

CONTENTS

Foreword — ix

Preface — xiii

Acknowledgments — xvii

CHAPTER ONE
From the Quarterdeck to the Classroom:
Naval Education Comes to Annapolis — 1

CHAPTER TWO
Leaving Port:
Franklin Buchanan Gets the Naval
School Under Way — 19

CHAPTER THREE
Navigating through the Shoals:
George Upshur's Ordeal at the
Naval School — 47

CHAPTER FOUR
From Naval Academy to National Institution:
The Stribling Years, 1850–53 — 73

CHAPTER FIVE
Toward a Naval Profession:
The Superintendency of Louis M. Goldsborough — 101

CHAPTER SIX
Officers and Gentlemen:
The Annapolis Ideal   133

CHAPTER SEVEN
Summer Cruises   165

CHAPTER EIGHT
Into the Maelstrom:
The End of the Old Naval Academy   181

Epilogue   197

Bibliography   203

Index   209

FOREWORD

Charles Todorich and I met years ago as colleagues on the Naval Academy's history faculty. I was then, in my spare time, researching my history of the Academy, and Lieutenant Todorich was pursuing postgraduate studies at the University of Maryland. One of his papers, which he generously placed at my disposal, was a survey of the antebellum academy. His interest in the subject has now resulted in this account, as entertaining as it is authoritative, of the crucial, opening years of the school "by Severn's shore."

The history of the Academy may be divided into four periods. The first spanned the years from 1845 to 1861. It began when Secretary of the Navy George Bancroft resorted to bureaucratic subterfuge to cut the Gordian knot of congressional and professional opposition to any such institution. It ended when the outbreak of the Civil War led to the Academy's removal to Newport, Rhode Island. This is the period covered by *The Spirited Years*. The second period, following the Newport interlude, began with the Academy's return to Annapolis under the dynamic superintendency of Vice Admiral David Dixon Porter in 1865. It extended through the naval doldrums of the 1870s and 1880s to the renaissance of the 1890s. Two events in 1898 initiated the third phase: the war with Spain, which gave America an overseas empire to defend and which helped confirm the steel navy's commitment to the Mahanian doctrine of command of the sea; and the decision to rebuild the Academy's antiquated plant according to the architectural plan of Ernest Flagg. This period, continuing through the two world wars, was one of dramatic growth, during which the expansion of the

Academy's facilities and student body paralleled the rise of American naval power. The fourth, and present, period, started with the first small step away from the traditional fixed curriculum in 1958. Since then, the Academy has seen the introduction of a full-fledged majors program, the admission of women, a marked increase in the role of civilian faculty, aggressive recruiting of minority-group members, the first major construction since the completion of the Flagg plan, and a loosening of the regulations governing midshipmen life.

Of all these periods, the first was by far the most fractious. The Naval School, as it was called and in which classes opened on 10 October 1845, bore only a rudimentary resemblance to today's Academy. The Yard, a former army post, encompassed only nine acres. Faculty and staff consisted of the superintendent, two officer instructors, and four civilian professors. Midshipmen in attendance, some of whom were billeted in what had been the post bakery, numbered fifty-six. The course of instruction was for two years, interrupted by a required two-and-a-half-year stint at sea. Depending upon the needs of the navy, the midshipmen might also be ordered to sea at any point in the academic year. Ashore, the program was almost wholly devoid of military content. The midshipmen were not drilled, inspected, or organized into any sort of formation. They did have to stand tours as duty officer; otherwise, their responsibilities were limited to attending classes, behaving in a manner befitting gentlemen, and not absenting themselves from the Yard without authority.

Over the next fifteen years, great changes occurred. The size of the faculty and student body more than quadrupled, the Yard's original nine acres grew to sixty-five, and many buildings were erected. More important than the increase in scale, however, was the evolution of institutional purpose. The curriculum was extended to four consecutive years, the at-sea experience to be provided by annual summer cruises. The school—officially and indicatively renamed the U.S. Naval Academy in 1850—developed a distinctly military character. The midshipmen were organized into units commanded by upperclassmen who were held accountable for their juniors' appearance, discipline, and drill. By 1860, the Naval Academy had become a military institution.

How this transformation came about is the theme of *The Spirited Years*. The reader will discover it was not a tranquil passage. As would-be heirs to the rollicking ways of sailors ashore, many midshipmen did their best (or their worst!) to resist the efforts of successive administrations to impose the discipline and training necessary to make the Academy more than a school. Incidents of drunkenness, duelling, and insubordination and an antic disregard for unwelcome regulations bedevilled all early superintendents; the second of them finally confessed his inability to govern his "young gentlemen" and implored them, in vain, to govern themselves. By the close of the period, however, authority and good order had prevailed.

Much of this story has never before been told. In the 139 years of its existence, the academy has been the subject of numerous books, but remarkably few have been histories. Four were published between 1862 and 1900; the next, excluding a centennial pictorial, did not appear until 1979.[1] All these are general surveys. *The Spirited Years* is the first in which modern research methods have been applied to describe a particular—and a particularly eventful—period of the academy's history. A glance at the bibliography makes clear that the author has left no source untapped. In addition to examining all the pertinent books, articles, and dissertations, he has consulted the primary materials in the National Archives, the Naval Academy Archives, and the Special Collections Division of the Nimitz Library. Notable among these materials are the superintendents' letter books, the journals kept by the Academy's duty officers, the after-action reports of midshipmen summer cruises, and the fascinating manuscript history of the academy written in 1887 by former faculty member Thomas G. Ford.

The results of this research are presented in a fast-paced narrative which places a definitive history of the antebellum Academy in the context of nineteenth century American education. Readers familiar with the modern academy may be surprised to see how many of the problems and tensions that emerged during this era remain of concern today. Of special interest to students of military sociology will be the analysis of the origins of antebellum midshipmen, here used to test the provocative thesis of Peter Karsten's *The Naval Aristocracy.*

As one who has been both a student and a teacher at the Naval Academy, Charlie Todorich writes with a deep insight into the nuances of its corporate life. He also writes with a wry wit, one example of which is his characterization of Commander Louis M. Goldsborough, the academy's fourth superintendent, who stood six-feet-four and weighed close to three hundred pounds, as "a St. Bernard of sea dogs."

I wish I had written that!

JACK SWEETMAN

[1]Edward Chauncey Marshall, *History of the Naval Academy* (New York: D. Van Nostrand, 1862); [Lieutenant Commander Edward P. Lull], *Description and History of the Naval Academy from its Origin to the Present Day* (n.p.: 1869); James Russell Soley, *Historical Sketch of the United States Naval Academy* (Washington, D.C.: Government Printing Office, 1876); Park Benjamin, *The United States Naval Academy* (New York: G.P. Putnam's Sons, 1900); and Jack Sweetman, *The U.S. Naval Academy: An Illustrated History* (Annapolis, Md.: Naval Institute Press, 1979).

PREFACE

The last history of the Naval Academy to cover only its antebellum years was Edward Chauncey Marshall's *History of the Naval Academy* published in 1862. Writing when he did, Marshall, a former West Point instructor, could accomplish the ever since impossible task of covering the Academy's entire history and its first sixteen years with one stroke of the pen. By necessity, subsequent histories have devoted increasingly smaller percentages of their space to these early years. And that is unfortunate because the years between its founding in 1845 and its move to Newport, Rhode Island, at the outbreak of the Civil War are among the most interesting and colorful in the history of the School.

They are also among the most important. It was during this period that the efficacy of formal naval education ashore was proven; that the authority of the superintendent over the daily affairs of the School was established; that the Academy became the near sole supplier of officers to the fleet; that the tradition of civilian professors as teachers of naval officers was maintained; that the Academy's Executive Department emerged as a kind of a police force; that midshipmen were transformed from quasi-officers to student-cadets; that the Academy developed a broad-based college-like curriculum; that a mutually beneficial relationship between the Academy and the town of Annapolis began; and that the Academy became a repository for navy memorabilia and tradition. In short, the foundations of the modern Naval Academy were laid in these antebellum years at Annapolis. These are some of the themes covered in this book that early Academy chroniclers could not fully appreciate. Neither could they know that the

Old Naval Academy had produced some soon to be famous names—Mahan, Dewey, and Sampson to name a few. Justification enough, perhaps, for a new look at the Old Naval Academy.

Ironically, this new look was aided most by the one early Academy historian whose work has gone unpublished for over a hundred years. Thomas G. Ford was the Naval Academy's assistant librarian from 1855 to 1866, in which capacity he collected material of all kinds on the Academy's early years and combined it with his personal knowledge of the school to produce a manuscript of considerable length, detail, and insight. The manuscript was still unfinished when Ford left the Academy in 1866 to return to Newport, Rhode Island, and so it remained for several years. He finally enlisted the aid of Stephen B. Luce who was unable to convince the Appletons of New York to complete and publish the manuscript. Neither was Luce able to "interest some brilliant young graduates of the Academy in the matter." In 1889, Ford sent the manuscript to Academy Superintendent Commander William T. Sampson who had the manuscript type-copied and passed on to his successor, Captain Robert L. Phythian. It was reviewed by the Academy's Library Committee who gave it high marks but said that only the author "was fitted to complete it for publication." Still no publisher could be found, and several years passed. In 1900, Academy Superintendent Commander Richard Wainwright informed Ford via Luce that he wanted a copy of the manuscript in the library "until some officer might be found willing and able to prepare it for publication." In the meantime, Park Benjamin's *History of the Naval Academy* had appeared, and Ford neglected Wainwright's request. In 1905, Luce finally persuaded Ford to send the manuscript to Academy Superintendent Rear Admiral James H. Sands, and not long thereafter the U.S. Naval Institute supposedly printed some fifty copies of the first three chapters, but nothing more came of it. Thomas G. Ford died in Florence, Italy, in 1909.

The Ford Manuscript now reposes in the Special Collections Division of the Nimitz Library, and it has been of immeasurable value to this researcher. By using it in combination with the superintendents' letter books and the other early Academy records on file at both the National Archives and the Naval Academy Archives, as well as almost all of the available secondary materials, I have been able to produce, in some cases, an almost daily account of school life during these early "spirited years." It reveals to a far greater degree than other books the magnitude of the Old Naval Academy's discipline problems—especially drunkenness—and how they were handled by the various superintendents of the period. We learn much about the midshipmen, officers, and professors of the Old Naval Academy—why they came, what they thought, and to what they aspired. *The Spirited Years* attempts to do more than tell the superficial story of when new buildings were constructed, superintendents rotated, or new courses added. I've tried to dig beneath the veneer to get at the sum and substance of Naval Academy education and to place this experience against the backdrop of American life and higher education in the antebellum period. This I believe will be the major contribution of *The Spirited Years* to Naval Academy historiography.

A surprisingly large portion of this historiography has been the product of the Navy community. In fact, almost all of the general histories of the Academy have been written by either an Academy graduate, an Academy instructor, or a naval officer. I was each of these in the fall of 1975. It was the fact that I was also a part-time graduate student in history at the University of Maryland that provided the impetus to undertake this project. What began with some research into old Naval Academy letterbooks at the National Archives became a course paper on life at the early Naval Academy. Another paper soon followed and some years later my master of arts thesis. And now this book. It has been a long voyage and it is appropriate that the University of Maryland had a hand in this first modern history of the Old Naval Academy. The two schools, after all, share a common historical thread in the personage of Franklin Buchanan—from 1845 to 1847 the first superintendent of the Naval Academy and from 1868 to 1869 the president of the Maryland Agricultural College, the forerunner of the University of Maryland. That "fearless man of action" would, I believe, be pleased that a graduate of the two schools with which he had been closely associated is telling this story. And so would Thomas G. Ford.

ACKNOWLEDGMENTS

I once heard a publisher attribute the production of his monthly magazine to "a series of well-timed coincidences." In my case, I must give credit for the publication of this book to the help I received from many fine people. It is my pleasant task to acknowledge them here.

Were it not for my four years as an instructor in the History Department at the Naval Academy, I would have had neither the opportunity nor the stimulation to undertake this project. I am indebted to Professor John W. Huston, History Department chairman at that time, for providing me this opportunity and for his counsel over the years as a teacher, colleague, and friend. Several other former History Department colleagues deserve thanks as well. Ken Hagan stimulated my interest early on in naval education and was a thoughtful, provocative commentator on some of my initial drafts. Jim Bradford, now at Texas A&M University, read and commented on several chapters as they evolved over several years and has provided the encouragement and support one comes to expect from a true friend. It was also my good fortune to have Jack Sweetman as a colleague and friend over these years. As perhaps the leading expert on Naval Academy history, Jack has been an invaluable source of information of all kinds, and I am honored that he agreed to write the Foreword for *The Spirited Years*.

My research was made easier by the help of several people from the staffs of the National Archives, the Nimitz Library, the Naval Academy Archives, and the Naval Institute. Of special help were Dr. Cary Conn, National Archives; Mrs. Jane H. Price, Naval Academy Archives; Miss

Alice S. Creighton and Miss Pamela Sherbert of Special Collections, Nimitz Library; and Mrs. Patty M. Maddocks of the Naval Institute.

Thanks go also to my indefatigable typist, Mrs. May A. Crasnick of Portland, Maine, and to Mr. David Eckard who reproduced several of the photographs used in this book.

My two editors at the Naval Institute, Cynthia Barry and Deborah Guberti, provided all the good advice and help that a first-time author needs, and I am deeply grateful to them.

At a time when the institutions of education and family have been under strain I have been fortunate to have the best of both. My mother and father have always been everything one could ask of parents, and my wife, Patty, has endured years of my late-night work, not to mention research notes strewn about the house for weeks on end. As for education, I am indebted to the many fine teachers of the Johnstown, Pennsylvania, public school system during the 1950s and 1960s, and to my professors in history at the Naval Academy. In similar vein I want to acknowledge the contributions of Professors David F. Sparks, E.B. Smith, and the late Walter Rundell, all of the University of Maryland, for their excellence in the classroom and for their commentary on this manuscript.

Of Walter Rundell a few special words. During my several years of graduate study at Maryland he was my academic advisor and valued friend. He died shortly before I received word of the publication of this manuscript. I can say without equivocation that were it not for Professor Rundell's high standards and consummate professionalism, *The Spirited Years* would have never gotten beyond the level of a course paper. To him I owe one of the very fine moments of my life.

THE SPIRITED YEARS

CHAPTER ONE
FROM THE QUARTERDECK
TO THE CLASSROOM:
NAVAL EDUCATION COMES
TO ANNAPOLIS

On a spring evening in 1846 Annapolis society thronged to the old theatre on the Duke of Gloucester Street to witness Bulwer's *Lady of Lyons* performed by the midshipmen of the newly established Naval School, as the Naval Academy was then called. The first performance of the play had been so well received that the midshipmen were emboldened to exercise their histrionic talents once again, but this time without a ban on "grog" behind the scenes. The play proceeded smoothly until interrupted by the familiar sound of popping corks backstage, after which the actors "became highly charged with spiritual electricity which sparked in every word and gesture."[1] Annapolitans howled and School officials scowled. The play climaxed when the villain excoriated, with unusual force, the reunited lovers, crying, "Curses on ye both! May thorns be planted in the marriage bed." Luckily the play ended before force became farce. Shortly thereafter the old theatre was torn down to make way for a Presbyterian church, leading one midshipman to claim that the "heathenish rites" of the cast were responsible for the spread of religion in Annapolis.[2]

[1]Thomas G. Ford, "History of the Naval Academy," 1887 unpublished manuscript in the Special Collections Division of the U.S. Naval Academy Library, Annapolis, Md., Ch. 10, p. 13 (hereafter referred to as the Ford Manuscript).

[2]United States Naval Academy Graduates Association, *First Annual Reunion* (Baltimore: Press of Isaac Friedenwald, 1887), p. 12.

Academy-founder George Bancroft and Fort Severn as it appeared in 1845. Anybody who suggested at its establishment the future vastness of the Academy "would have been thought a dreamer." Courtesy: U.S. Naval Institute Collection

If so, these early midshipmen were unlikely disciples—more often found in taverns than in temples, more prone to settle personal disputes with duels or fisticuffs than with the golden rule, and more concerned with physical courage and personal honor than with piety. Even the *Lady of Lyons* incident pales in comparison with later midshipmen escapades, such as hanging instructors in effigy, burning down the outhouse, tunneling under the Academy wall into town, and tarring and feathering a classmate. These early men of Annapolis posed a formidable challenge to those charged with molding them into educated officers and polished gentlemen, and the infant Academy often bore little resemblance to a military or educational institution. Yet, by 1851 the present format of a four-year course of instruction with summer cruises had emerged, and the School was renamed the Naval Academy. The Civil War saw Annapolis graduates distinguish themselves as junior- and middle-grade officers. Many of these same officers, in the role of gunboat diplomats and explorers, were agents of American commercial expansion overseas in the 1870s and 1880s. The professionalization of the navy's officer corps continued in 1884 with the founding of the Naval War College by Stephen B. Luce (Naval Academy Class of 1849). In 1890, Alfred Thayer Mahan (Class of 1859) published *The Influence of Seapower Upon History, 1660–1783*. Mahan's book fanned the growing navalism that produced the bluewater battleship navy that was commanded during the Spanish-American War by George Dewey (Class of 1859), William T. Sampson (Class of 1861), and Winfield S. Schley (Class of 1860). All the while, the Naval Academy and Annapolis worked a special synergy on each other; the by-passed port city became the cradle of the navy, and the one-time naval school grew into a national institution. Thus, the *Lady of Lyons* had provided only the first of many roles for the midshipmen who were part of the life and times of the Old Naval Academy.

The Old Navy

The founding of the Naval Academy was one of several events that marked the passing of the Old Navy. Beginning with John Paul Jones, the story of the Old Navy is that of a succession of single-ship encounters in which sturdy Yankee ships and their heroic crews duelled all who would sully American honor. Men like Truxton, Preble, Perry, Porter, Bainbridge, Hull, and Decatur and ships like the *Enterprise, Essex, Philadelphia, Constellation*, and *Constitution* came to symbolize a young nation whose pugnacity far exceeded her power. Like knights-errant, America's sea captains were quick to rile, always ready to fight, and never willing to surrender.

The story of Captain James Lawrence and the *Chesapeake* is a good example. Bottled up in Boston by the British blockade during the War of 1812, Lawrence took offense at H.M.S. *Shannon*, a 38-gun frigate that was parading back and forth across the entrance to Boston Harbor. Despite his orders to avoid the blockade in order to raid British commerce in the Gulf of St. Lawrence, James Lawrence took his still-green crew and an unready *Chesapeake* to answer *Shannon*'s challenge. In a battle that lasted just fifteen minutes, the British captured the *Chesapeake* and mortally wounded Lawrence whose delirious dying words, "Don't Give Up The Ship," became legend. The true account of the action was offered by the British captain who reported, "The enemy made a desperate but disorderly resistance."[3]

While adhering to the single-ship tradition at sea, the Old Navy did have *some* organization ashore, especially after the War of 1812. In 1815 Congress provided for a three-man Board of Naval Commissioners to advise the secretary of the navy on professional matters. Composed of senior naval officers appointed by the president, the board proved useful at first but eventually came to represent conservatism in a service that begged for reform. Because the secretary retained control over naval policy and operations, the commissioners were relegated to administering the navy's shore installations, further isolating them from the service afloat and making them into a "peremptory triumvirate which never lost an opportunity of overruling the opinions of even the most skilled and experienced constructors."[4]

The ships of the Old Navy were divided into squadrons (the Mediterranean, West Indies, Brazil, Pacific, and East Indies) which protected American commerce around the world. On the navy's lists in 1816 were five 74-gun ships of the line, five 44-gun frigates, and thirty-one smaller ships totaling 588 guns. By 1842 the navy listed fifty-six ships mounting 2,002 guns, including one 120, ten 74's, and fourteen 44's. A tiger on paper, the American navy was more of a pussycat at sea, since many of its ships were either decommissioned or never completed. With sails, smoothbores, and wooden hulls rapidly becoming relics, the ships that the Old Navy did have were technologically out of date. Moreover, the navy lacked any "fleet consciousness," adhering instead to the single-ship concept of sea power. With a languishing navy and her eyes riveted West, America relied on the expanse of the Atlantic, harbor fortifications, and an aroused citizenry to secure her coast in time of war.

A huge gulf separated officers from the enlisted ranks. Wretched living conditions, dangerous work, low pay, and brutal discipline were the sailors' lot, and many found solace in their daily half-pint of grog. While grog

[3]E. B. Potter, ed., *Seapower—A Naval History* (Englewood Cliffs, N.J.: Prentice-Hall, 1960), p. 213.

[4]*The Commodores*, quoted in Kenneth J. Hagan, ed., *In Peace and War* (Westport, Ct.: Greenwood Press, 1978), p. 80.

soothed some sailors, it stimulated others to breaches of discipline that were answered by flogging. The life of Jack Tar appealed to few Americans in this age of the common man, and many foreigners manned the navy's rails.

If the seamen of the Old Navy were its serfs, then the officers were its nobles, and the commodores its kings.[5] "The typical commodore of the Old Navy was a law unto himself . . . a most austere and august personage, bluff, proud, pompous, reserved, and self-willed."[6] As commanders of distant squadrons, commodores were invested with extraordinary powers to conduct diplomacy and wield force in support of American economic interests. Just as junior officers were jealous guardians of their personal honor, the commodores were quick to answer affronts to the national honor. Given their responsibilities, their distance from home, the threat of piracy, and the nature of naval combat that often saw fighting at close quarters, the officers of the Old Navy were well-suited to their tasks. Their premium on physical courage and personal honor was well placed, and it outlived the passing of wooden ships.

On land, however, the special qualities of its officers rendered a navy "rent by cliques."[7] In the second most famous duel in American history Commodore James Barron killed Commodore Stephen Decatur, and for years the navy was divided between Barrons and anti-Barrons. Commodore Oliver Hazard Perry questioned Captain Jesse Elliott's courage at Lake Erie, and the two families feuded for thirty years. That the navy was dominated by great naval clans like the Perrys, Elliotts, and Rodgers's only complicated matters. The scales of naval justice were weighted heavily in favor of senior officers, whom juniors accused of being aristocratic and conservative. Old Navy officers were no band of brothers.

The problems in the navy's commissioned ranks reflected its near total lack of standards for the selection and education of officers and for weeding out the unfit. Midshipmen appointments were the prerogative of ship captains, the secretary of the navy, and the president. Political influence counted heavily.[8] Samuel F. Du Pont received his appointment after his grandfather wrote to President Jefferson, while Thomas McDonough,

[5]Harold D. Langley, *Social Reform in the United States Navy, 1798–1862* (Urbana, Ill.: University of Illinois Press, 1967), p. viii.

[6]"The little tyrant . . . who struts his few fathoms of scoured plank," according to David Porter. Charles O. Paullin, *Paullin's History of Naval Administration 1775–1911* (Annapolis: U.S. Naval Institute, 1968), p. 191. From a series of articles originally published in the *U.S. Naval Institute Proceedings* between 1905 and 1914.

[7]Ibid., p. 195.

[8]A throwback to the British. At one time British admirals were allowed to have fifty servants in the ratings of midshipman, tailor, barber, fiddler, footman, and steward. Since these ratings were often stepping-stones to a commission in the Royal Navy, the admirals had quite a power of patronage.

Matthew Fontaine Maury, and Daniel Ammen enlisted the aid of influential congressmen. Stephen Decatur and David Farragut received their appointments from captains, Farragut at age nine.[9] Benjamin F. Sands was appointed through his uncle's connections with navy secretary Samuel L. Southard, and ordnance expert John A. Dahlgren used the recommendations of various members of the Pennsylvania legislature to secure his warrant. Not until 1831 were appointees required to be able to read and write well and to understand grammar, arithmetic, and geography.

As late as 1842, Secretary of the Navy Abel P. Upshur admitted that he appointed those applicants with the "best" recommendations.[10] An increasing number of southern secretaries beginning in the 1820s produced a southerly migration of the geographical center of the officer corps. Whereas New England had once supplied most of the navy's officers, by 1842 44 percent of midshipmen appointments were from Maryland and Virginia.[11] Charles O. Paullin, an early chronicler of the navy, writes, "The most important factor in the selection of midshipmen was political and personal influence; and many statesmen of the older times left memorials of their families in the navy list by making midshipmen of sundry sons, grandsons, nephews, and cousins."[12]

Since competition for appointments was keen, candidates without good recommendations stood little chance. In March 1835, 2,355 applications were on file when the navy already had 200 more midshipmen than it needed.[13] Romance, prestige, escapism, a desire for security—these were the motivations of most of the applicants. A few were sent to sea because they were misfits on land. Of them, Secretary of the Navy Upshur wrote:

> . . . wayward and incorrigible boys, whom even parental authority cannot control, are often sent to the navy as a mere school of discipline, or to save them from the reproach to which their conduct exposes them on shore. It is not often that skillful officers or valuable men are made out of such material. The belief, heretofore prevailing, that an officer of any standing in the navy could not be driven out of it, or at least that he could not be kept out of it, has a strong influence in ruining its discipline and corrupting its morals and manners.[14]

[9]During the War of 1812, the twelve-year-old Farragut acted as prize master of the captured *Barclay*, making him the youngest person ever to command an American vessel.

[10]Henry L. Burr, "Education in the Early Navy" (Ph.D. diss., Temple University, 1939), pp. 43–46.

[11]Samuel P. Huntington, *The Soldier and the State: The Theory and Politics of Civil-Military Relations* (Cambridge: Harvard University Press, 1967), p. 214.

[12]Paullin, *Paullin's History*, p. 194.

[13]Ibid., p. 195.

[14]Henry F. Sturdy, "The Establishment of the Naval School at Annapolis," *U.S. Naval Institute Proceedings* 72 (April 1946): 4.

An 1820-era midshipman (left). Little formal training existed, as midshipmen were more captains' errand boys than officers in training. Courtesy: U.S. Naval Institute Collection

Many midshipmen were court-martialed, but because of their political connections few were dismissed from the service. The pattern often continued as a commissioned officer when promotion backups produced lobbying in Congress for rank that harmed discipline and challenged the authority of the secretary of the navy. Membership in the Old Navy often had little to do with ability and performance, and there was much truth in the statement that a "cruise in Washington was worth two around Cape Horn."[15]

Naval education was flawed as well. An Act of Congress in 1813 authorized schoolmasters for 74-gun ships of the line, of which there were then none. Even when built, the 74's were seldom able to employ superior teachers, for the pay was only $25 a month.[16] In 1807, a school for midshipmen was started at the Washington Navy Yard and others at Boston, New York, and Norfolk after 1825. Attendance was voluntary, and therefore poor, and the last of the Navy Yard Schools was dismantled in 1839. Thus, a midshipman lucky enough to be on a 74 or able to attend school ashore might receive rudimentary instruction in mathematics, navigation, and languages. Others received no instruction at all. Consequently, the navy boasted few officers of any real scientific or intellectual attainment prior to the 1830s. One aged Neptune could not understand why magnetic variation was applied to the right of the compass needle when entering the Mediterranean and to the left when leaving, and he nearly lost his squadron on the coast of Africa as a result. Another considered navigation to be the secret of the captain and the master and forbade midshipmen to determine longitude. As Samuel R. Franklin stated, "The whole system of naval education in those days was rough and crude, and did not seem altogether fair; the wonder is that we got on as well as we did."[17]

The Old Navy, then, was a preprofessional organization, unable to regulate its members or their conduct, lacking an adequate system of education, and uninterested in making a science of the art of war. It reflected the Jacksonians' distrust of a professional officer corps which smacked of the British, particularly the Royal Navy. Thus, Congress refused to authorize the rank of admiral until the Civil War. In so doing, Congress slowed promotion and doomed its haughty commodores to the

---

[15]Langley, *Social Reform*, p. 23.

[16]This was about half as much as professors' yearly salaries at schools like Dartmouth ($600 in 1805); Georgia ($600 in 1815); and Bowdoin ($700 in 1825). Professors at South Carolina in the 1800s and Virginia in the 1820s earned $1500 yearly. Those at Harvard during the 1830s received $2000. From Frederick Rudolph, *The American College and University: A History* (New York: Alfred A. Knopf, 1962), p. 193.

[17]Samuel R. Franklin, *Memories of a Rear Admiral* (New York: Harper and Brothers Publishers, 1898), p. 90.

gave his consent on 16 June. Meanwhile, the Naval Board of Examiners was meeting in Philadelphia and on 13 June Bancroft requested its opinion regarding a school at Annapolis. By presenting the establishment of the school as a fact and consulting the board only with respect to its nature and location, Bancroft deftly sidestepped opposition within the navy. After debating for twelve days, the board recommended Annapolis as the location, largely because of the influence of Captain Isaac Mayo, an Annapolitan.

On 25 June the board submitted its conclusions to Bancroft. Besides Annapolis as the site, it recommended:

(1) that a grade of naval cadets from 13 to 15 years of age be created and appointed in the same manner as West Point cadets

(2) that a practice frigate and a small steamer be located at the school

(3) that the program include two years of study at the school followed by three years at sea and then a year at the school aboard the practice frigate before the lieutenant's exam

(4) that, except for the abstruse study of calculus, the course of study be almost identical to that of West Point

(5) that the school's Academic Board, assisted by three persons appointed by the secretary of the navy, conduct annual examinations of the midshipmen.

According to the examiners, "by making this grade [Naval Cadet] the source from which all others shall spring, and by imposing on it acquirements of a comparatively high character, most of the delinquences now so common in the Navy would be unknown, when the system shall have been thoroughly incorporated into the service."[30]

The examiners' proposals were soon reinforced in a separate report by Passed Midshipman Samuel Marcy who, along with Professor Lockwood, had just returned from a first-hand study of West Point. They, too, advocated that the West Point program, which costs "less. . . than any of our seventy-fours in commission," be used as a model for the naval school to "enable our officers to keep pace with the improvements in the sciences ultimately connected with the profession."[31] While they might blush in admitting it, Annapolites owe no small debt to their earlier cousins on the Hudson and their considerable influence on early Naval Academy history. In Annapolis, rumors of the naval school were fanned by the visit of Bancroft, Secretary of War Marcy, and Commodore Lewis Warrington on 15 July for the purpose of inspecting Fort Severn. Finally, on 5 August

---

[30]Ford Manuscript, Ch. 8, p. 21.
[31]Ibid., p. 12.

Marcy assented to the transfer and on 15 August Fort Severn was officially transferred to the Navy Department.

With Fort Severn in hand, Bancroft circumvented Congress once again and acquired funds for the school by discharging half of the navy's twenty-two mathematics instructors and using the money to set up the school. As one source writes, "The civilian teachers of the Navy thus left coldly on the beach were, willy nilly, the financial benefactors and founders, the Leland Stanfords and Ezra Cornells, the John Harvards and the Eli Yales of the Naval School at Annapolis."[32] On 7 August, Bancroft charged Commander Franklin Buchanan with establishing the school, and on 3 September Buchanan assumed command. Lockwood, Chauvenet, Ward, and Marcy were appointed the school's first instructors, and the first of many generations of midshipmen found their way to Annapolis. At 11:00 A.M. on the morning of 10 October 1845, the instructors and midshipmen gathered in one of the recitation rooms to await the remarks of Commander Buchanan that would, at long last, officially open the Naval School.

[32]Carol H. Foster, "The United States Naval Academy," *Scribner's Magazine* 64 (July 1918): 8.

CHAPTER TWO
LEAVING PORT:
FRANKLIN BUCHANAN GETS
THE NAVAL SCHOOL UNDERWAY

Many nineteenth-century American naval officers won greater fame than Franklin Buchanan. A few surpassed him in professional achievement. But none could boast of a career more interesting and varied, more full of challenges well met, than this greatest of the pre–Civil War Academy superintendents. Franklin Buchanan, born the son of a Baltimore physician in 1800, had a lifetime interest in good society, the affairs of Maryland, and the sea. At the age of eight he moved to Philadelphia which during the War of 1812 would have as its heroes Commodores James Biddle and Stephen Decatur. Here the young Buchanan fell under the sway of the "martial spirit" of the period. The burning of Washington, the bombardment of Fort McHenry, Francis Scott Key's "Star Spangled Banner," the romantic achievements of American frigates and their stalwart captains against the British—all of these factors led to Buchanan's becoming a midshipman in 1815 at the age of 14.[1] (Francis Scott Key was, in fact, a brother-in-law.) He served aboard the *Java* under Oliver Hazard Perry, did a year and a half stint with the merchant marine in the Far East, returned to naval service against the Caribbean pirates, made two long cruises to the Mediterranean, advanced to the rank of lieutenant in 1825, and captained the 64-gun ship *Baltimore* on its delivery to Brazil in 1827, before finally being assigned duty ashore in Philadelphia. Buchanan

---

[1] Charles Lee Lewis, *Admiral Franklin Buchanan: Fearless Man of Action* (Baltimore: The Norman, Remington Co., 1929), pp. 11, 14.

Commander Franklin Buchanan. Foremost among the Academy's antebellum superintendents, Buchanan fought in the Mexican War, commanded Perry's flagship in the opening of Japan, and sided with the Confederacy during the Civil War. Courtesy: U.S. Naval Academy Archives

threatened by wind off the Severn that swept through cracks around windows and doors. Heat was supplied by wood, later by anthracite coal. Twenty tons were delivered to the School soon after the new year. The first group of midshipmen paid for their own fuel and lighting, while those present at the beginning of the second year requested that the government meet these expenses. Three hundred and fifty dollars annual pay could only reach so far, and the request was granted. Stewards attended to the midshipmen's rooms.[30]

The midshipmen's mess was run by one Darius King. King Darius, as he was called, was an emancipated black man with a long reputation as an able wardroom steward.[31] Feeding a hundred midshipmen on twelve dollars a month each, however, was beyond his abilities. His "alternate fits of economy and extravagance" played havoc with his budget, not to mention the digestive powers of the midshipmen. When Commander Buchanan once complained of the number of eggs being consumed, Darius swore that Midshipman Ochiltree had eaten twenty in one day. Thereafter, the "Egg Order" set the limit at two a day. The classic description of Darius is Thomas G. Ford's:

> Darius always appeared in the Mess-hall with a cheerful and confident air when the bill of fare was unobjectionable in form and substance, but on other occasions he prudently remained in the kitchen. Many a time did he open his larder to midnight marauding parties of Midshipmen, of whom he stood in dread, and rarely could be induced to betray them. In fact, he was their best friend, but alas, reefers are proverbially ungrateful to cooks and stewards. Darius in one of his economical fits served up a succession of ancient ox-joints and patriarchal turkeys, and a leader at one of the tables passed the word for the guilty caterer to appear, and in an instant every Midshipman in the hall shouted "*Darius*" in stentorian tones. In those days there was no officer in charge to suppress such a tumult, and so Darius with slow and faltering steps obeyed the summons. On entering the hall, the disjecta memba of the ancient gobblers were held up to his terrified gaze with appropriate comments, and then hurled at his head from every table with volleys of bread balls and other missiles at hand. For a while, Darius manfully breasted the storm, shielding his most vulnerable part

[30]Sarah Corbin Robert, "The Naval Academy as Housekeeper: Feeding and Clothing the Midshipmen," *U.S. Naval Institute Proceedings* 72 (April 1946): 120.

[31]Another prominent black man at the School was Moses Lake. He presided over the barbershop from the School's opening until the Civil War "with a grace and urbanity peculiar to himself." Ford Manuscript, Ch. 16, p. 39. A lesser-known black was Dennis. Hired as a "boy" in 1845, he worked at odd jobs at the Academy for about sixty years, well into the 1900s. Dennis, then, brushed shoulders with veterans of the War of 1812 like Buchanan, as well as the likes of King, Spruance, Nimitz, and Halsey who made their marks one hundred thirty years later.

from the flying projectiles; but the rapid and accurate fire of his assailants compelled him at last to beat a hasty retreat. Numerous were the troubles of this King of the Kitchen during the five years of his reign, and when he abdicated in 1850, he regarded his successor with feelings of the deepest commiseration. He died soon afterwards in debt, but in the odor of sanctity, leaving behind him a name still cherished by numerous descendants.[32]

Darius's downfall is surprising, for Buchanan had gotten him to the School only after considerable effort. After Darius's arrival, the governor of Maryland informed Buchanan of an 1831 Maryland law that prohibited free Negroes from entering, or being hired in, the state. On 7 October, Buchanan wrote U.S. Attorney General John Y. Mason (the next secretary of the navy) for an opinion as to whether Maryland had the authority to enact such a law. In his response of 30 October, marked "Unofficial," Mason ventured that Maryland had acted within its authority. Meanwhile, on 9 October, Buchanan had requested that Darius be sent to the School as a landsman in the service of the government for a wage of one cent a month, the midshipmen's mess paying the rest of the salary. This arrangement was approved and Darius stayed on.[33]

CONGRESS ACCEDES

Buchanan's hard work at Annapolis during the summer and fall of 1845 paid off in Washington in December when Congress convened and was confronted with a new shore school for naval officers. Secretary Bancroft let the truth be his sword. The School, he argued, was a big improvement over shipboard and shipyard schools. Moreover, it required no increase in appropriations, being merely a more judicious use of existing funds. Bancroft's forthrightness defused opposition in Congress, which the next year provided $28,200 "for repairs, improvements, and instruction at Fort Severn, Annapolis, Maryland."

The holiday season also brought a welcome leave for the midshipmen, and a Grand Naval Ball upon their return. Organized by one Midshipman Edward Simpson, the ball "produced a flutter among the fair sex"[34] that

---

[32]Ford Manuscript, Ch. 10, p. 1.

[33]Washington, D.C., "Records of the Naval Academy," Record Group 405, National Archives (hereafter referred to as "Records of the Naval Academy"). It is interesting that Buchanan, a southern sympathizer, tried to circumvent a state law under the guise of national authority. He was not the first man of his era with logic tortured by the slavery question.

[34]Thomas G. Ford claims that the army had only moderate success with local ladies in its stay at Fort Severn, but "the introduction of naval tactics proved more potent in subduing the hearts of the ladies. If they could not be won by a sailor's blarney, [then] a lace shawl or a

brought ladies from as far as Washington, Baltimore, the Eastern Shore, and even New York. The barracks became a "temple of Terpsichore" as uniformed middies and their maidens danced to the music of the Marine Band, which Buchanan had obtained.

With acceptance in both Annapolis and the halls of Congress, Buchanan had good reason to be pleased. In his first quarterly report to Bancroft on 30 January, he spoke approvingly of the school and its students. The midshipmen, he said, were well behaved when absent from the school and highly regarded by strangers. Though it was not yet on open seas, the young Naval School was finally leaving port.

Buchanan's Midshipmen

The midshipmen under Buchanan's command were a disparate lot. The younger, newly appointed acting midshipmen were called "youngsters." Although seven youngsters were ordered to the opening session of the School, only three had arrived by 10 October. Besides passing an entrance exam, these boys had to be between thirteen and sixteen years of age, of good moral character, and free of any defect, disease, or infirmity that would "disqualify [them] from performing the active arduous duties of a sealife."[35] If successful in their studies after a year at the school, they would be sent to sea for a six-month trial period preparatory to receiving their midshipman's warrants. After two and a half years at sea, they would return to the School for a year's study for the lieutenant's exam. These youngsters were raw material of a sort, the first to receive an Annapolis stamp. Fuzz-faced and fresh from puberty, they offered themselves up to the School to be molded into proper officers for the navy. In return they received in varying degrees the wages of the profession—prestige, rank, adventure, travel, fame, danger, responsibility, loneliness, boredom, injury, and death. One can wonder at the thoughts of these young boys as they contemplated their new prospects. Theirs would be a life far different from that of friends back home. And for many in 1845, home was days, even weeks, distant. It was an early age and a tough way to become a man.

Already grown men were the "oldsters," a group of senior midshipmen who ranged in age from eighteen to twenty-seven years. Having entered the service between 1840 and 1842, they were detailed to the School for a year's study prior to their lieutenant's exam. In these days, midshipman status usually lasted six years, thus a man of the Date of 1840 could hope for

---

family of canaries from Madeira, a Spanish mantilla, a straw bonnet from Leghorn, a velvet cloak from Genoa, a silk dress from Lyons, a box of gloves from Paris, or an amber necklace from Constantinople was used with telling effect." Ford Manuscript, Ch. 10, p. 8.

[35]Lewis, *Admiral Franklin Buchanan.* p. 95.

Boyish-looking Midshipman Francis S. Conover. A disciple of Edward Simpson,
Conover authored the "Spirit Song," the lusty rendition of which marked the
Spirits Club's frequent "meetings" in Annapolis taverns. Courtesy: U.S. Naval
Academy Archives

lieutenancy in 1846, those of the Date of 1841 in 1847, and so on.[36] In theory they were pupils. In reality they "regarded themselves . . . as officers on leave of absence from sea duty. Consequently, the most military exercise was duelling, the most popular uniform dressing gowns, and the favorite study researches into the spiritual possibilities of barley and the grape."[37] Here were men a far cry from those who enter the Academy today. Many were bearded and had visited salons in London and Paris, had fought in Calcutta and Gibraltar, and had met pashas and princes in the East. Having been quasi-officers at sea, they were reluctant to abide by strict rules ashore. Try as they might, they were not typical college freshmen. As one observer writes, "For a while they toed the mark of discipline with commendable meekness, but by degrees the student yoke began to be felt severely, and the victims sought consolation in such amusement as the old provincial town of Annapolis afforded."[38]

While Annapolis was not Constantinople, it had its attractions. Harry Matthews's tavern was a favorite spot for a group of the 1840s known as the Spirits.[39] Limited to nine members, they went to the tavern every Saturday night for supper of oysters and terrapin. They were led by their Grand Master, Midshipman (later to be Rear Admiral) Edward Simpson. While Harry Matthews kept a sharp lookout for School brass, Simpson, with the assistance of Deputy Grand Master Midshipman Richard Aulick, would brew the Spirits' special whiskey punch. An evening of imbibing was closed with Simpson leading his cohorts in a lusty rendition of the "Spirit Song."[40] The Spirits were popular in town and their transgressions winked at by Buchanan, even when on one night they collected the city's oil lamps and piled them in front of the Gate House. They wore with pride a square gold badge with the Greek letters Zeta, Ro, and Sigma (representing fried, roasted, and stewed oysters) on three corners, and the Roman letter *S* (for Spirits) on the fourth. A figure of a turtle, symbolic of secrecy, graced the center of the badge.[41]

More attuned to the Jacksonian spirit of their time than the aristocratic Spirits of Apollo Row were the Ballsegurs, a loosely organized group mostly

---

[36]As it turned out, the Date of 1840 midshipmen finished in June of 1846. The large Date of 1841 followed and was split, its sections attending the School between 1847 and 1850. The Date of 1842 graduated along with the 1841 group, but formed a separate class. There were no midshipmen of the 1843 and 1844 dates, which was just as well, for the School had all of the oldsters it could handle.

[37]Foster, "The United States Naval Academy," p. 8.

[38]Ford Manuscript, Ch. 10, p. 3.

[39]"A colored gemman of the old school, who was proud of his larder stocked with all the delicacies of the Chesapeake . . ." Ford Manuscript, Ch. 10, p. 4.

[40]The song was composed by Midshipman F. S. Conover.

[41]Ford Manuscript, Ch. 10, p. 6.

from Rowdy Row. Their exploits included whitewashing the government horse, tarring the clapper of the School's bell, and firing the signal gun from their quarters with the aid of a lanyard. Commander Buchanan's "war speeches" seldom identified the offenders, partly because of the "prudently feigned ignorance" of the watchman and the group's practice of not betraying its members. Strangely enough, this did not preclude duelling between members who, with their seconds and a surgeon, would steal across the Severn to Fort Madison for the exchange of four shots before breakfast. As Thomas G. Ford notes, "A steadier hand or a quicker eye on one of those cold mornings would have perhaps affixed an indelible stain upon the earliest history of the Naval School."[42]

The Winter of Buchanan's Discontent

Mixing worldly oldsters and precocious youngsters with the drab, cloistered, academic life of the Naval School was bound to cause problems. On 1 February, barely two days after his quarterly report praising the midshipmen, a chagrined Buchanan wrote to Bancroft recommending a court-martial for Midshipman Nones who, restricted for academic deficiency, left the yard without permission. As this was the first instance of "so flagrant an offense,"[43] Buchanan felt that an example should be set. Bancroft agreed and sent Nones packing within three days.

Several days of calm followed the Nones dismissal. Then came the incident with Midshipman McLaughlin. Buchanan had authorized McLaughlin to visit his ostensibly sick mother in Baltimore. When Buchanan spotted him playing billiards in Annapolis, McLaughlin lamely explained that the barracks servant had failed to awaken him, causing him to miss the train. It was apparent that McLaughlin had been drinking, in violation of an earlier promise of sobriety. In his 17 February letter to Bancroft urging a court-martial, Buchanan said that McLaughlin was one of the few midshipmen who had problems with "dissipation." Bancroft dismissed him from the School saying, "No drunkard should be tolerated in the navy. The School is not to be a hospital for incurables, but a school for selected young men."[44] The "few" others, however, quickly appeared, and on 19 February Buchanan once again found himself reporting intoxicated midshipmen to the secretary, this time Whitlock and Blake. The latter was delirious and required the aid of Surgeon Lockwood. After Christmas leave and January parties, the midshipmen were rebelling against the dreary routine of school

[42]Ibid.

[43]Buchanan to Bancroft, 1 February 1846, "Records of the Naval Academy."

[44]Buchanan to Bancroft, 17 February 1846, "Records of the Naval Academy." The midshipmen petitioned Bancroft to restore McLaughlin, but the secretary stood firm.

life. The drinking problem now appeared in larger dimensions to Buchanan. He wrote to Bancroft:

> . . . dissipation is the cause of all insubordination and misconduct in the Navy, and will, if countenanced by me under any circumstances at this School, ruin its usefulness to the service . . . and injure its character with the country.[45]

Buchanan's leniency quotient, never great, was now exhausted. On 27 February he suspended two midshipmen (one of them Edward Simpson) for smoking in their room, a fairly minor offense. Meanwhile, Bancroft officially reprimanded Whitlock and Blake. This was serious punishment in those days when personal honor and reputation counted for so much. The frequency of drinking incidents decreased to one each in March, April, and May. The Bancroft–Buchanan team had prevailed. But the underlying problems of the youngster–oldster mix, substandard quarters, and an unrealistic academic work load plagued the School for years. Other secretary–superintendent teams would face the same problems of midshipmen misconduct that resulted, but none as well as the first. It may be that David Dixon Porter performed the best service in this regard by instituting organized athletic competition at the Academy when he became superintendent in 1865. Midshipmen could now vent their frustrations on each other.[46]

The First Examinations: A Report Card for the School

With the coming of spring, the smell of peach blossoms and fresh Chesapeake air wafted through rooms lately stale with smoke from the cigars of Edward Simpson and other midshipmen—now busily preparing for end-of-year examinations. The School's Academic Board examined the junior class of eight acting midshipmen in April and reported its rankings to Buchanan.[47]

---

[45]"Records of the Naval Academy."

[46]Walter Aamold, "Naval Academy Athletics—1845–1945," *U.S. Naval Institute Proceedings* 72 (April 1946): 105.

[47]A brief note on the fate of these eight midshipmen. Hayes died in 1849, Hamilton resigned in 1860, Houston died in 1860, McKean resigned in 1847, Adams was dropped from the navy's rolls in 1851, Goodloe resigned in 1846, and Smith resigned in 1853. Only Ralph Chandler, whose aptitude for the service was rated as "ordinary," enjoyed a naval career that included the Civil War years and beyond. He was promoted to captain in 1874. From Thomas H. S. Hamersly, ed., *General Register of the United States Navy and Marine Corps (1782–1882)* (Washington, D.C., 1882).

Table 2-2. The First Midshipmen Grades

Name	Mathematics	French	English	Nat. Philos.	Chemistry
Wm. Bainbridge Hayes	8	9	9	8	6
Jno. Randolph Hamilton	7	8	7	6.5	6
Thos. Truxton Houston	7.5	6	6	8	8
Franklin Buchanan McKean	5.5	5.5	5.4	4	5
John Adams	4	5.5	5	4	5
Ralph Chandler	4	4	5	5.5	5
John Jas. Goodloe	5	3	5	5	0
Wm. Henry Smith	3	3.5	2	3	2

They were also graded in more subjective areas.

Name	Aptitude for the Service	Habits of Study	Deportment at Recitation
Hayes	Good	Good	Correct
Hamilton	Good	Rather Good	Not Correct
Houston	Good	Good	Correct
McKean	Good	Idle	Frequently Inattentive
Adams	Ordinary	Idle	Inattentive
Chandler	Ordinary	Fair	Correct
Goodloe	Little	Idle	Bad
Smith	Very Little	Not Bad	Inattentive

Additionally, the midshipmen were categorized as Good, Indifferent, or Bad with respect to their chances of surviving the upcoming examination ("ordeal," as Lieutenant Ward put it) of fitness for service by the Board of Examiners. That board would also examine the senior class for promotion to passed midshipman prior to lieutenancy. It was an ordeal for these oldsters, too, as Midshipman Jeffers wrote on 10 May:

> I yesterday took an account of my studies, already passed over, in order that I might commence to review them. Hitherto I have been preparing for recitations; now I commence to prepare for examination in dead earnest. The sum total consists of 2,750 pages, part of which is to be read; a part to be studied, making a daily average of fifty pages, independent of the regular studies of the day. I have, therefore, bidden adieu to all my friends

without the walls, and, until the fiery ordeal shall have been passed
through you must expect no more letters from me.[48]

In fact, the Board of Examiners was coming to examine the whole
concept of naval training ashore. Here was to be the School's first report
card. Bancroft determined it would not be the last. No mean politician
himself, he carefully selected the membership of the board which included
Commodores Lawrence Kearny and Matthew C. Perry, and Captains
McKeever, McCauley, and Mayo. Mayo had been instrumental in selecting
Annapolis as the site for the School, and Perry had long advocated reform in
naval education. Bancroft gave the board its instructions on 19 June, and it
arrived in Annapolis the next day. The guidelines were tough, but realistic:

> . . . as this is the commencement of a new system of education in the
> Navy, a failure in any one branch other than Seamanship and Navigation is
> not to *reject* an officer, provided he passes high in those branches. Hereaf-
> ter, the midshipmen will be required to pass in all the branches taught at
> the School.[49]

Rejected midshipmen were to be considered unfit for the service. Those
who merely failed to pass and who had good aptitude for the service could
stay at the School and be examined the next year. Two-time failures would
be removed from the service. Bancroft also directed the board to examine
the junior class, though more cursorily than the senior, and to report to him
the conditions and means of improving the School. It was a tall order, and,
fittingly, when the board convened on 22 June the first order of business
was a prayer by Chaplain Jones.

The examinations emphasized practical knowledge. Most were written,
but seamanship was oral. The midshipmen might be asked to "recite the
line of battle," to "rig lower yards," to "draw a gun and name its different
parts," or to "measure a vertical angle." Letters from commanding officers
and journals from past cruises counted, too.[50] So did not being in debt. On 4
May, Bancroft had ordered Buchanan to determine the status of midshipmen's debts in town prior to exams to emphasize frugality and honor. This
policy prevailed throughout the period before the Civil War.[51] In all,

---

[48]Elihu S. Riley, "Early Days," 213. Jeffers graduated fourth of forty-seven in his class.
[49]Board of Examiners Reports, "Records of the Naval Academy."
[50]Ibid.
[51]In some years, the midshipmen would just be asked if they had the means to pay their
debts. In other years, as in 1849 when thirty-five of thirty-six midshipmen examined had
debts, payment was a prerequisite to passing the exam. Even so, some fourteen midshipmen
left the School without paying their debts. Seven of them had a combined debt of $657.26.
Midshipman Carter accounted for $254.88 of this, a substantial sum by 1849 standards.

forty-three oldsters passed the exam, three were rejected, and three were ordered to return to the School in the fall.[52] The acting midshipmen were examined and ordered to sea.

Despite their gravity, examinations did have some lighter moments. One of these involved Professor Girault. Born as Arsene Napoleon Alexandre Girault de San Fargeau in Troyes, France, in 1801, he was the only man of foreign birth on the first faculty. The midshipmen later nicknamed him Mr. Frog. His father had been a wealthy contractor for the armies of Napoleon, the professor's life-long hero. His family's finances ashambles, Girault emigrated to the United States in 1826 and became a French teacher. He wrote several French texts, one of which he used at the Naval School where in September 1845 he had been appointed "temporary Agent of the Navy for teaching French."[53]

Girault appeared before the examiners to examine Midshipman Nelson who, despite the professor's efforts, had not acquired a command of conversational French. Instead, Nelson had memorized only a few common French phrases in preparation for the exam, which went like this:

GIRAULT: Mr. Nelson, which is your native state?

NELSON: Thank you, I am very well.

GIRAULT, now glaring: What cruise have you just finished?

NELSON: I am about twenty-four years old.

The grilling went on, but Nelson had a different phrase for every question fired by Girault. The professor was infuriated, but Commodore Perry was impressed. He ended the ordeal by congratulating Girault on Nelson's fluency in French.[54] It is fortunate that Perry was sent to open Japan and not Paris. The midshipmen had their revenge in other ways as well. One of the Date of 1841 tied together the coattails of two examiners known to dislike each other. They never discovered the perpetrator.[55]

[52]Two men, Richard Aulick of Virginia and Robert Savage of North Carolina, tied for first place among the oldsters and cast lots to break the deadlock. Aulick won.

[53]Lewis, *Admiral Franklin Buchanan*, p. 105.

[54]Leland P. Lovette, *School of the Sea: The Annapolis Tradition in American Life* (New York: Frederick A. Stokes, 1941), p. 76.

[55]Ford Manuscript, Ch. 11, p. 31. The examiners and their wives were quartered at the home of Mrs. Green on Church Circle, the site of the present executive mansion. Their daily march to the School was "quite a show," with more brass and gold braid than Annapolis had seen since George Washington resigned his commission there. The examiners and their wives were "great sticklers for rank." Spotting this pompous procession one morning, a little boy said, "Here comes the Commodores." An officer's wife corrected him in a loud voice, "No my little fellow, only Commodore S. and the Captains." From P. H. Magruder, "A Walk Through Annapolis in Bygone Days," *U.S. Naval Institute Proceedings* 55 (June 1929): 513.

Professor Arsene Girault. As unusual in appearance as he was talented, Girault taught French and Spanish. The midshipmen called him Mr. Frog. Courtesy: U.S. Naval Academy Archives

A PASSING GRADE AND THE PASSING OF BANCROFT

The examiners made their report to Bancroft on 11 July. They praised Buchanan's administration of the School and endorsed his recommendations for the construction of additional faculty and midshipmen quarters and recitation rooms; the setting aside of two hundred to three hundred dollars a year for experimental apparatus and additions to the library (then at 350 volumes); and the stationing of a brig at the school for a practice ship. The board also recommended sending a few rowboats to the School for midshipmen recreation which

> . . . would doubtless have a tendency to divert the young gentlemen from a practice of mingling too generally in the society and amusements of the Town, by which their minds are distracted from their studies, and expenses fall upon them, which their pay is inadequate to meet.[56]

With a good report card in hand, Bancroft made ten thousand dollars of recently appropriated funds immediately available to Buchanan to provide accommodations for one hundred midshipmen. He also ordered the revision of the School's regulations so as to make them the result of "practical experience, simple and comprehensive, without being unnecessarily numerous."[57]

On 9 September, Bancroft left the Navy Department to become ambassador to England. Only once, in 1878, did he visit the Academy. He devoted his life to politics, diplomacy, and literary affairs, dying in 1891 at the age of ninety. Bancroft's lifetime work as a historian brings him little recognition today, his various works collecting more dust than readers. He is remembered instead as the founder of the Naval Academy, and when the School was rebuilt in the early 1900s it included the world's largest dormitory, Bancroft Hall, home for the four thousand members of the Brigade of Midshipmen.

War

While Buchanan and Bancroft could take pride in the School, their thoughts were likely elsewhere, for on 13 May war had erupted with Mexico. Over the winter, President Polk had dispatched John Slidell on a secret mission to Mexico to negotiate a solution to the Texas question and to buy New Mexico and California. Thwarted by a revolution in Mexico, Slidell came home in March empty-handed. Meanwhile, in January, Polk had ordered Taylor to the Rio Grande. Skirmishes occurred there in May

---

[56]Board of Examiners Reports, "Records of the Naval Academy."
[57]Bancroft to Buchanan, 13 August 1846, "Records of the Naval Academy."

Professor Henry H. Lockwood. The bespectacled professor was second in influence only to Chauvenet among the Academy's early instructors. He commanded the midshipmen in infantry drill and, as a brigadier general, led a brigade at the Battle of Gettysburg. He had a "homespun demeanor" but a "will of iron." Courtesy: U.S. Naval Academy Archives

before a 'sojer'."[27] Drill was not only too military, it was "landlubbery,"[28] and the midshipmen purposely complicated the professor's task, which they likened to pig driving. Whereas Lockwood's orders were crisp, brisk, commanding—the students' response was to slouch, stand on one foot, and shuffle. They dismantled his guns, hid the parts, and threw the linchpins into the Severn River.

Still, Lockwood persisted and on the afternoon of 21 March 1848, the midshipmen held the first "demonstration" in Naval Academy history. They assembled in the lower part of the yard amid cheers and shouts of "down with gunnery." This rebellious proceeding was quickly broken up by Lieutenant Lee, but the midshipmen's work had only begun. That night they placed insulting placards throughout the yard and hanged Lockwood in effigy. Next morning, the School and Annapolis awakened to the sight of a man suspended from the School's flagstaff some forty feet off the ground in full naval uniform with thin spectacles and a model gun attached to his arm.

George Upshur was outraged. He dashed off a classic letter to Secretary Mason.[29]

> United States Naval School
> Annapolis, Md.
> 24th March 1848
>
> Sir,
> I am greatly pained and most deeply mortified by the necessity of reporting a most reprehensible act which occurred at this School on the afternoon of the 21st and which was followed at a late hour on the morning of the 22nd by a disgraceful outrage and gross violation of Naval law and discipline admitting of no apology.

Upshur went on to call the incident the "greatest outrage I have ever known committed under Naval or Military rule," and concluded with these remarks on discipline at the School:

> I have counselled, advised, persuaded, lectured, suspended and reported, and you have reprimanded and finally ordered offenders to sea. The last expedient has had an excellent effect upon a large majority, but the desired object has not yet been fully attained. A few cases of prompt dismissal from the service would, I doubt not Exercise a most salutary and permanent influence over the future government of this School, and should it be the pleasure of the Department to order the trial of the officers herein

---

[27]Benjamin, *The United States Naval Academy*, p. 183.

[28]Richard S. West, Jr., *Admirals of American Empire* (New York: Bobbs-Merrill Company, 1948), p. 17. The distaste for marching endures among present-day midshipmen.

[29]Upshur to Mason, 24 March 1848, "Records of the Naval Academy."

named, I would most respectfully, but earnestly recommend, that the sentence of the Court, whatsoever it may be, should be promptly carried into effect and never reversed.

> I have the honor to be Sir,
> Most respectfully
> Your: Obedient: Servant:
> G.P. Upshur
> Commander & Superintendent

At Upshur's urging, the ringleaders had already come forward so as to relieve their innocent classmates of the "odium" and wages of guilt.[30] The three of them, Midshipmen John M. Murphy, E.H. Scovell, and John Gale, were arrested and charged with insulting a superior officer. But Lockwood was not an officer and, to undercut the trio's belated defense on these grounds, Secretary Mason acted through Congress and made civilian professors officers in the navy with a four hundred dollar increase in pay. The aggrieved Professor Lockwood, along with Chauvenet, had traveled to Washington to assist Mason in this task. This prompted the midshipmen to remark "that for such an increase in pay Lockwood could afford to be hanged in effigy every year," and they turned his horse loose in Annapolis—painted like a frigate and with a lantern hanging from its head. They were unaware that the good professor had interceded at the Navy Department on behalf of their three arrested brethren.[31]

The perpetrators by now realized the gravity of their offense and, in a 31 March letter, requested a personal audience with Mason. The secretary rebuked them for bypassing Upshur in the chain of command and denied the request. A naval court-martial that included Commanders Franklin Buchanan and David Glasgow Farragut convened on 17 April and deliberated for several weeks before rendering a guilty verdict. On 13 May, in the presence of the assembled midshipmen and staff, Upshur carried out Mason's orders and dismissed Murphy, Gale, and Scovell from the service.[32] Still, Lockwood's ordeal was not over. As he was marching his unwilling troops toward the Severn River one day, he tried to order them to "Halt." But with his stutter, he only managed a series of "Haw, Haw, Haw's," and into the river went the midshipmen, dutifully but gleefully pulling the guns behind them.

---

[30]One of the midshipmen offered to "give the professor such satisfaction as he might desire or such as was usual among gentlemen," in effect challenging Lockwood to a duel.

[31]Ford Manuscript, Ch. 11, p. 32.

[32]Scovell was later readmitted to the School and then kicked out again for rude treatment of Upshur, who had recommended reinstatement in the first place. Murphy, also given a second chance by Upshur, graduated from the School, and resigned from the Service in 1864.

MIDSHIPMAN DUELS

While they abhorred Lockwood's version of it, the midshipmen did espouse their own form of gunnery—duelling. The institution of duelling had a glorious history in the navy. Between 1798 and 1848, thirty-three naval officers were killed in duels that resulted from "jealousy, factionalism and an exaggerated sense of honor."[33] The Decatur-Barron duel in 1820 was the most famous. Legend had it that no officer had ever refused a challenge. In the Old Navy if a midshipman sat down at the mess table in short sleeves, it was considered an insult requiring the offender to fight a member of the mess. A Lieutenant Richard Somers once fought three duels in one day, and in 1840 two future admirals, David D. Porter and S. C. Rowan, nearly duelled when Porter stuck his divider points in a table. President Andrew Jackson once dismissed three lieutenants from the service for duelling a Philadelphia doctor. Still, Jackson refused to halt duels "between officers whose profession was fighting, and who were trained to arms."[34] Of course, Old Hickory himself had engaged in several duels. Strange as the idea of settling disputes with pistols at ten paces seems today, these "affairs of honor" were almost obligatory to those of the eighteenth or nineteenth century who demanded retribution for some personal affront, however slight. In some instances, the range of the duel was so close that the outstretched arm and cocked pistol of each antagonist passed inside that of the other. Though theirs was a fool's courage, Old Navy duellists were men of real grit. Given the role of the navy in protecting the national honor and the fact that naval warfare in those days often involved action at close quarters including boarding, grappling, and hand-to-hand combat, it may be that this type of officer was unavoidable, even necessary.

For the duellists, the experience could be physically and psychologically overpowering. And it must have been thoroughly exhilarating, for the stakes were ultimate—the drama highly personal. It was like a manhood rite—the challenge, the act, the satisfaction—almost sexual in its connotations. One can only wonder at these men's thoughts at a dawn encounter as they stepped off the distance in measured pace, took their aim, and squeezed off a shot. Those who fired first and missed knew a special kind of horror. If ever there was a heart-thumping blood-rushing, spine-tingling experience, it was the duel.

The first of the 1848 duels took place behind the bowling alley near the fort just after supper on the evening of 4 May. The participants, Midshipmen Walter W. Queen and Byrd A. Stevenson, chose to fight on the

[33]Langley, *Social Reform*, p. 24.
[34] Benjamin Franklin Sands, *From Reefer to Rear Admiral* (New York: Franklin A. Stokes, Co., 1899), p. 40.

light of their recent misconduct, he feared they would misbehave and embarrass the School. The midshipmen were enraged and spent the nights of the 5th and 6th of March ringing ship's bells, firing guns, and blowing tin horns they had bought in town.[46] On 11 March, the midshipmen broke into Upshur's office. This was all reported by the superintendent in a 15 March letter to the new secretary of the navy, William Ballard Preston. It was an appropriate introduction to the School for Preston.

The sorry saga of the spring of 1849 continued when the watchman found Midshipman Whitaker, recently of Barnum Hotel, lying on the ground, drunk and begging for help. Two more midshipmen, one in a "state of helpless intoxication," were reported drunk on 14 June.[47] In July, it was not boozing but brawling that plagued Upshur. A fist fight had erupted between Midshipmen Simmons and Van Wyck. They were separated by Midshipman Scovell, of all people. Upshur demanded promises from the two pugilists that they would not fight a duel. Simmons declined and was suspended. Van Wyck, however, agreed. Still, Upshur felt compelled to warn Preston that Van Wyck's pledge not to duel would expire upon detaching from the School. By this time Preston must have been somewhat immunized from the daily disaster reports arriving from Annapolis. One can only guess at his reaction to the 8 August conduct list that ranked Van Wyck in the "excellent" column and contained this comment by George Upshur: No officer at the School, claimed Old Put, had ever "ventured to contest my orders" or "treated me with disrespect."[48]

The School Becomes an Academy

But events were already at work that would bring the midshipmen to heel. Professor Chauvenet and the Academic Board again urged the adoption of their 1848 plan for the reorganization of the School to the Board of Examiners that convened in the summer of 1849. In his 17 August letter to the examiners, Upshur made the formal request for "the appointment of a Board or mixed commission of sea officers and professors to revise, correct, amend and extend the rules and regulations for the government of the School . . . ." The examiners, which included former Superintendent Franklin Buchanan, endorsed the proposal and further recommended that the new regulations conform with those of West Point, whose graduates

---

[46]One of the midshipmen involved was Stephen B. Luce, whose class standing was dropped from fifth from the top to tenth from the bottom because of the incident. Luce founded the Naval War College in 1884. The War College's first lecturer was Alfred Thayer Mahan.

[47]Upshur to Preston, 14 June 1849, "Records of the Naval Academy."

[48]Upshur to Preston, 8 August 1849, "Records of the Naval Academy."

had performed with such distinction in the Mexican War. According to General Winfield Scott, "but for our graduated cadets, the War . . . . might, and probably would, have lasted some four or five years."[49]

On 4 September, Secretary Preston, sensing the growing strength of the School's supporters, appointed a Board of Officers to reorganize the School. Besides Upshur and Chauvenet, this Board of Revision included Commodore William B. Shubrick, Commanders Franklin Buchanan and Samuel F. DuPont, and Surgeon W. S. W. Ruschenberger. Just a few weeks later, the superintendent of West Point, Captain Henry Brewerton of the U.S. Army Corps of Engineers, was added as a consultant on discipline. The board convened in Washington on 1 October and made its report to Preston on the fourteenth. On 1 July 1850, after several months of delay and the further urging of these officers, Preston put the new plan into effect.

The 1850 reorganization was, and still is, the most significant development in the history of the School. The course of instruction was extended from one year of study to four. The first two years were to be at the School, followed by three years at sea, and then two more years at the School. Entrance exams would be given once a year in October, and the new midshipmen would not receive their warrants until after their first six weeks at sea. The lieutenant's exam followed successful completion of the last two years of the course.

With the School's future less uncertain, there was no longer a need for the secretary of the navy to oversee its daily administration. Hence, the School was placed under the Bureau of Ordnance and Hydrography, although the superintendent still reported to the secretary on disciplinary matters. The superintendent was also made president of the Academic Board. The executive officer became the new commandant of midshipmen with responsibility for instructing in naval tactics and seamanship. The commandant ranked below the superintendent and above the professors and instructors who were department heads. The next rank down consisted of assistant professors and officer instructors. Rank among midshipmen was according to their date of appointment to the school.

There were now six departments of instruction: naval tactics and practical seamanship, mathematics, natural and experimental philosophy (science), gunnery and infantry tactics, ethics and English, and modern languages. The professors, commandant, and superintendent comprised the Academic Board which administered annual and semiannual examinations. A new marking system that ranged from 0 to 4.0 was introduced, with 2.5 needed to pass.

[49]Ford Manuscript, Ch. 11, p. 19.

The grading standards were tied into a new system of demerits as part of a larger effort to improve the discipline and military order at the School. Under the old system, demerits consisted of small subtractions from the final merit marks in the various courses. Now, a separate grade for conduct, weighted equally with mathematics, was to be factored into the final class standing. The conduct grade was based on the number of demerits a midshipman received. Anyone who accumulated two hundred demerits was subject to dismissal. Demerits were to be awarded for violating any one of the newly drawn regulations. Comprehensive and numerous, these regulations aimed at giving the new School a character much different from the old. Many were keyed to eliminating some of the more common midshipmen evils. Entertaining in midshipmen's rooms, visiting during study hour, cooking in rooms, forming clubs or "convivial associations" in town, using tobacco, profanity, contracting debts, duelling, playing cards, bringing liquor onto the grounds, and visiting hotels and taverns in town without permission—these were but some of the activities now prohibited, the last four by pain of dismissal.

The effect was to put clubs like the Owls, Crickets, Spirits, Ballsegurs, and others out of business and to place "reform banquets" outside of the law. The Board of Revision even went so far as to recommend that the Maryland legislature make it unlawful for townspeople to extend credit to the midshipmen or to encourage any of them to violate the School's regulations. One midshipman from each room was to be designated super-intendent of the room for a week and was responsible for its orderliness.[50] The superintendent or commandant was now charged with making daily inspections of the dormitories, recitation halls, and grounds. All of the School's personnel were required to report infractions to the superintendent, and all, even the officers and professors, had to obtain the superintendent's approval to leave the grounds. Midshipmen liberty was restricted to Saturday afternoon until 8:00 P.M. (9:00 P.M. in the summer). Civilian clothes were prohibited and a new uniform was devised for the acting midshipmen. They wore a cap like the midshipmen, but their jacket differed in not having buttons on the cuffs and pockets. The cap also lacked the gold lace band of the oldsters.[51] To the dismay of the midshipmen, the Navy Department's rule on hair, beards, and mustaches was held to apply to Annapolis, too.

[50]The origin of the present ICOR (In Charge of Room) system.

[51]This was the uniform until 1855 when the double-breasted jacket with rolling collar and gold anchors was introduced. The jacket was worn unbuttoned, with a silk neckerchief providing a "nautical touch." The working jumper also appeared in 1855. Seniority was indicated by the number of turns of blue braid on the jumper: First Class, 3; Second Class, 2; Third Class, 1; Fourth Class, 0. Lovette, *School of the Sea*, pp. 77–78.

Mandatory formation also began in 1850, as the midshipmen were organized into gun crews and companies for infantry drill. A hierarchy among the midshipmen was set up with each gun crew headed by a first captain. The companies marched in battalion under the stern eye of Professor Henry H. Lockwood, assisted by the two highest ranking midshipmen—the adjutant and assistant adjutant.[52] Having been hanged in effigy only two years earlier, the mere thought of his own battalion surely warmed the old professor's heart.

Affairs of the heart, though, were now forbidden the midshipmen by a new regulation prohibiting getting married while at the School. Deprived of both romance and beards, the midshipmen felt they were being made into machines. Thomas G. Ford notes that the rule caused "much unfavorable comment in domestic circles having a surplus of marriageable daughters but some of these got to windward of the order by tying up their lovers in vows that even salt water could not always weaken."[53]

The midshipmen were now given a chance to see salt water during the summer, for a practice ship—a sloop of war—was promised to the School. This was in line with the aim of making Annapolis similar to West Point, which had a summer encampment for the cadets. Also like West Point, a new Board of Visitors composed of senior officers and headed by the chief of the Bureau of Ordnance would make yearly inspections of the School.

Finally, to make the West Point analogy complete and to reflect the truly revolutionary nature of the changes just wrought, the Naval School was renamed the Naval Academy.

UPSHUR'S DEPARTURE

With the last of the date of 1841 midshipmen soon to be graduated, George Upshur was preparing to leave the Naval School after three years as superintendent. The Board of Examiners's report of 21 June 1850 to Secretary Preston praised Upshur's "judicious management" of the School, but in reality the reorganization was due to his ineptness in governing under the old system and to the reform efforts of the Academic Board. Upshur's most long-lasting contribution was in 1847 when he acquired for the School three lots that lay between Fort Severn, Scott Street, Northeast Street and the Severn River. His tour at the School expired on 1 July 1850 when he was relieved by Commander Cornelius K. Stribling and was dispatched to the Mediterranean station as commanding officer of the sloop *Levant*. On 3 November 1852, George Upshur died in Spessia, Italy, at the age of fifty-three.

---

[52]These midshipmen were the forerunners of the present system of "stripers."
[53]Ford Manuscript, Ch. 13, p. 5.

The history of the Naval School ends and that of the Naval Academy begins with the reorganization of 1850. The School had survived midshipmen hijinks, the Mexican War, George Upshur, and the assaults of enemies in the service and in Congress. George Bancroft, Franklin Buchanan, and William Chauvenet were the men most responsible for nurturing the concept of naval training ashore into a Naval Academy by 1850, although a final reorganization in 1851 was necessary. Its imperfections aside, the Naval School had weeded out incompetent midshipmen and had enhanced professionalism and efficiency in the service, giving its graduates "a loftier conception of their profession and of the obligations which the advancement with service imposed upon them."[54] The first generation of Annapolites was set loose in the navy whose destiny they would help shape for the next half century.[55]

---

[54]Ibid., Ch. 11, p. 22.

[55]Thomas G. Ford notes that one of the first positive results of the Naval School was to provide the Naval Observatory in Washington, D.C. with qualified officers. There they examined ships' logs and charted winds and currents. Many officers served aboard the commercial steamers of the new Collins Line to Liverpool.

several subsequent periods it was found that the condition could not be complied with.

The obvious remedy for this is to connect the two courses and to complete the theoretical education before sending him to sea . . . . Regardless of conditions it is very desirable that the Academy should be directly established by Congress and its leading feature possess the sanction of law.[7]

Thus, Stribling was asking that Congress formally establish the Naval Academy and etch the key features listed below in legislative stone:

(1) That appointees be between the ages of fourteen and sixteen and that they not be warranted as midshipmen and sent to sea before completing a *four-year course* at the Academy

(2) That hereafter all midshipmen appointments be made from the list of Academy graduates in the order determined by the Academic Board

(3) That the number of naval cadets (the proposed name for midshipmen candidates) be no more than twice the number of congressional districts

(4) That the superintendent receive the rank and pay of a post-captain on sea duty

(5) That a secretary be provided for the Academy

(6) That a practice ship be stationed at the Academy.

In Stribling's view the four-year course would not dampen the midshipmen's thirst for naval life, but would give them "that age and maturity which it is necessary he shall have to command others and at the same time will not carry him beyond that age at which sea influences stamp those peculiar habits which are held essential."[8] In a poke at Graham, Stribling further urged that the Academy be put under the administrative command of one of the navy's bureau chiefs so as "to relieve the Secretary from details, the delegation of which to a Bureau would, from the greater permanency of its chief, secure uniformity of action in respect to the Academy."[9]

Here was a series of bold proposals, as important in tone as in substance. Whereas only a few years ago its actions were conciliatory, if not timid, the Academic Board was no longer pulling its punches. As a result of their continuity of service, the professors were increasing their power at the Academy. Already, Chauvenet and Lockwood had outlasted two superintendents and three navy secretaries. Thus, while Stribling might speak of

[7]Tisdale, "A Cruise," p. 365–66.
[8]Ibid., p. 366.
[9]Ibid., p. 367. This move was supposed to have been accomplished with the 1850 reorganization, but it apparently had not been.

the promises of Secretary Preston, his information was only second-hand, and, like many other superintendents who were inexperienced in educational affairs, he usually bowed to the will of the board. In a larger sense, the letter bespeaks the growing power of the Naval Academy which, it must be remembered, was established five years earlier only by the subterfuge of George Bancroft. Putting the issue to Congress, many of whose members still opposed formal naval education ashore, might put the Academy at risk. But no one knew the politics of naval education better than Chauvenet and Lockwood, whose experience dated back to the school at the Naval Asylum. They correctly surmised that five years of successful operation coupled with the ever-growing financial investment it represented gave the Academy a momentum that would not be easily slowed.

Fortunately, Secretary Graham agreed with Stribling and the rest of the board. Yet, he was reluctant to go to the legislative route, hoping instead that the service would gradually accommodate itself to a four-year course. But the logic of four consecutive years was compelling. Better to complete an officer's theoretical education all at once than to administer it in a pair of two-year doses separated by three years at sea. Indeed, one of the Academy's constant headaches had been in dealing with midshipmen who found the transition from sea to school difficult.

The four-year course with summer cruises grew increasingly attractive. Sensing a change of heart in Washington, the Academic Board in July 1851 urged the adoption of its plan to Secretary Graham who instructed the Board of Examiners to consider it. The examiners, headed by Commodore David Conner and including Franklin Buchanan, recommended that the plan be adopted with only a few slight changes. Graham was also influenced by that summer's first successful midshipmen practice cruise and a July letter from Stribling who contended that even the Navy's "Old Salts" were coming to favor the four-year concept.[10]

Finally, on 15 November Secretary Graham gave his approval. On Christmas Eve of 1851 at 1:30 in the afternoon the new regulations were formally announced to the assembled personnel of the Academy which had assumed at last its present form. Thereafter, only candidates between fourteen and sixteen years of age could be appointed acting midshipmen. Those in the first year of study were designated fourth classmen—they would become known as plebes as at West Point. Those in the second year were third classmen, or youngsters. Third and fourth year students were second and first classmen respectively. Hence, the birth of the present class system. Midshipmen could move up to the next higher class at an acceler-

[10]Glasow, "Establishment of the U.S. Naval Academy," p. 15.

ated rate by passing their final examination at an early date.[11] And they were no longer referred to by the date of their appointment but rather by the date of their Academy "graduation," the first of which under the new system was in 1854. Only those who graduated from the Academy could receive a midshipman's warrant. Thus, Annapolis had become the sole supplier of officers to the fleet. With a few wartime exceptions, the Academy's monopoly on naval officers remained largely unbroken until 1925 with the establishment of the Naval Reserve Officers Training Corps. The approved plan called for a practice ship to be stationed at the school for summer cruises and gunnery practice. Finally, provision was made for second class midshipmen of good conduct to enjoy summer leave during the cruise of the practice ship.

The reorganization of 1851 was a major triumph for Chauvenet, Lockwood, and other long-time champions of the four-year course. Implementation of the plan, which followed so closely on the heels of the 1850 reforms, was, however, something of an administrative nightmare, for there were now three groups of midshipmen: (1) the pre-1850 oldsters; (2) those who entered under the 1850 plan; and (3) those who would enter under the 1851 plan. The Academy was faced with the dismal prospect of administering three separate academic programs. The problem was eased when the Date of 1850 midshipmen were ordered to sea after only one year of study just prior to the implementation of the new plan. In order that the Academy could supply graduates to the service at the earliest possible date, ten of the new fourth classmen were formed into an advanced class after the completion of the semiannual exams in February 1852.[12] And so, the Academy ended up with three separate programs after all. Thus, during the 1852–53 academic year there were eight midshipmen of the advanced—or second class (a loss of two)—twenty-three of the third class (a loss of fifteen), and fifty-seven new fourth classmen. In addition, two midshipmen of the 1846 date and twenty-seven of the 1847 date were completing their last year of study at the school prior to their final examinations. Only six of the advanced class graduated in 1854 by which time the class system was fully established.[13] The last of the oldsters passed through the school in 1856, finally leaving the Academy with but one course of instruction to administer.

---

[11]Alfred Thayer Mahan skipped plebe year in this way.

[12]Ford Manuscript, Ch. 13, p. 25. Ford was well acquainted with the need for midshipmen in the fleet. He had served on board the sloop *Levant*, eighteen guns, in the Mediterranean from 1853 to 1855 as clerk to the commanding officer. Because of a lack of midshipmen, he was also required to serve as captain's aid and interpreter in port.

[13]Ford notes that even though exams were not difficult, the new system weeded out midshipmen who were not of the "right stuff."

The 1851 reorganization was by far the most significant development during Stribling's superintendency. Both he and the Academic Board deserve great credit for instigating the four-year course and for administering it under difficult circumstances.

Improved Education and Training

The sound organization provided by the 1851 plan served to clear the Academy's decks for action in other important areas. Chief among these was the overall program of instruction. Now that it had a four-year course as at West Point and other American colleges, the Naval Academy set out to become their equal in the quality of education and training it offered. Progress in this area, unlike the building program or the reorganizations of 1850 and 1851, was slow and undramatic. But it was steady and it was cumulative, and while it would be some time before comparisons to Harvard and West Point would cease to be embarrassing, the Naval Academy was at least steering a course in their direction.

On the academic front, the number of departments increased from six to nine with the creation of the Department of Drawing in 1851, the splitting of the Department of Modern Languages into its French and Spanish halves in 1852, and the formation of the Department of Astronomy, Navigation, and Surveying in 1853. Of necessity, there were new professors as well. Edward Seager, who also drilled the midshipmen in fencing, headed the Department of Drawing. The new Department of Spanish was run by the dignified Professor Edward A. Roget, referred to as the "Don" by his students.[14] Professor J. H. C. Coffin took over as professor of pure mathematics thus freeing Professor Chauvenet to take charge of the new Department of Astronomy, Navigation, and Surveying. Another new face was that of William Fenn "Poppy" Hopkins. He graduated from West Point in 1825 and had taught there until 1835 shortly before resigning from the army. Already he had received an A.M. degree from Yale (1833), and he went on to become the principal of the Norfolk Academy in 1843, professor of natural sciences at Western Military Institute in Kentucky in 1846, and president of the Masonic University in Tennessee and professor of chemistry at William and Mary College in Virginia before coming to the

---

[14]William Oliver Stevens, *Annapolis: Anne Arundel's Town* (New York: Dodd, Meade and Company, 1937), pp. 252–53. Roget was a protege of Girault who, as early as December 1845, had recommended his being hired to teach foreign languages. Girault described him as "a gentleman, an excellent French, English, and Spanish scholar." "Records of the Naval Academy."

the president by the secretary of the navy who often was acting upon the recommendations of senior naval officers and others with political connections to the executive. The number of midshipmen had been limited to 48 in 1794, but rose to 350 in 1801, and reached 450 by 1809, whereupon the president was empowered to appoint at will. The system was easy to abuse and often was, and an inordinate number of appointments went to a small number of naval clans and prominent families. The advent of the spoils system politicized the process even more. Appointees were often "outrageously unfit,"[51] and Philip Spencer was only one of the more notorious rotten apples in the barrel.

Fittingly, it was in 1842, the year of the *Somers* mutiny, that reality began to make its way back into the appointment process. At the urging of Secretary of the Navy Abel Upshur, Congress limited the number of midshipmen to 262. In 1845, the Naval Appropriations Bill decreed that midshipman appointments should be apportioned among the various districts and territories according to their representation in Congress. In addition, appointees had to be residents of the state of their appointment. The number of midshipmen permitted was increased to 464 in 1848, and in 1850 came the proviso that no appointments could come from a district that already had two midshipmen in the navy.

From here it was but a short jump to Congress's (actually the House of Representatives) takeover of appointments in 1852. Besides being evidence of congressional power in an era of weak presidents, the 1852 Act testified to the growing success of the Naval Academy.[52] No longer did an appointment mean only a long and uncertain apprenticeship at sea; it now offered something resembling a college education. Congress had controlled appointments to West Point for some time and knew full well how to turn competition for a ticket to Annapolis to political advantage. Too well, in the opinion of Thomas G. Ford who called the act unconstitutional and "the greatest blunder ever committed in the administration of our Navy."[53] In the short run his point had some validity, for failure rates among midshipmen were exceedingly high throughout the 1850s. Of the fifty-seven men who entered Annapolis in 1854 with George Dewey, only fifteen graduated (Dewey was number five in his class). Still, the system did produce a George Dewey from Vermont, a William Sims from Pennsylvania, an Ernest King from Ohio, a Chester Nimitz from Texas, and countless others who might not have stood a chance in earlier times. Far from being a fiasco, the system of congressional appointment of midshipmen was one of the more signifi-

[51]Carol H. Foster, "The Requirements For Admission to the Naval Academy—An Historical Review," *U.S. Naval Institute Proceedings* 44 (February 1918): 348.

[52]Ford Manuscript, Ch. 13, p. 29.

[53]Ibid., p. 30.

cant reforms of the period and played a major role in transforming the Naval Academy from a finishing school for the elite to a national institution.

The School Gets a Band

While the school was on the way to becoming a national institution, it still lacked the means to play the national anthem. There had been talk of a band for the school under both Buchanan and Upshur, but nothing came of it. The school's musical activities in its early years consisted of little more than the regulation fife and drum, midshipmen drinking songs, and Sunday morning hymns.

It was the 1852 Board of Examiners that sounded the need for "a more rigid observance of those Military forms and ceremonies, which are so essential in the order and discipline of the navy."[54] Whether this served to drum up support for the band is not clear, but on 10 November 1852, Navy Secretary John P. Kennedy wrote to Commodore Charles Morris, chief of the Bureau of Ordnance and Hydrography, "The want of music at the Naval Academy is so evident that I deem it necessary to invite your attention to the organization of a Band, to consist of not less than twelve instruments to be directed by a leader or a Master."[55] Soon thereafter, Morris directed Stribling to form a band consisting of one master and eleven musicians.[56] Stribling chose as the master one P. Pfeiffer who promptly enlisted in the navy as a first class musician and took up the task of recruiting band members. Among his many prospects were one musician with a pulmonic disorder that kept him from blowing, another with just one eye, and a third who had enlisted without the permission of his wife and who was let go at her demand. Pfeiffer overcame these obstacles, as well as competition from the upcoming World's Fair in New York which had many musicians' jobs, and delivered his band to the school in May 1853. Such was the origin of the Naval Academy Band, which has become one of the school's permanent fixtures and whose stirring and martial strains have never failed to strike responsive chords in the hearts of midshipmen and Annapolitans alike.

[54]Board of Examiners to Secretary of the Navy, 10 June 1852, "Records of the Naval Academy."

[55]Secretary of the Navy to Commodore Charles Morris, Chief of the Bureau of Ordnance and Hydrography, 10 November 1852, "Records of the Naval Academy."

[56]The master was paid eighteen dollars a month, six of the musicians twelve dollars a month, and the other five ten dollars a month. The midshipmen and staff contributed twenty-five cents a month to purchase the band's instruments and to cover other expenses besides pay.

improved library. Academic performance improved throughout his administration, although the Academy was still more training school than educational institution. Summer cruises highlighted the professional program; training in steam propulsion lagged. Despite cutbacks in funding, Goldsborough oversaw the further expansion of the Academy's physical plant. All the while, navy dollars became increasingly important to the economy of Annapolis. The mold for the modern Naval Academy had been poured during Stribling's superintendency. Under Goldsborough, it began to jell.

Louis M. Goldsborough: "Sea Dog"

To describe Goldsborough's naval career is to describe his life. Born into a prominent Maryland family in 1805, he received his midshipman's warrant in 1812. He did not see actual service until 1816. He was commissioned a lieutenant in 1825 just before taking a leave of absence to study at the Sorbonne in Paris, where he developed the intellectual breadth that made him such a capable superintendent. Thomas G. Ford describes Goldsborough as

> the first scientific officer appointed to the command of the Academy [and] in fact, one of the most brilliant officers of his rank or age in the service— a fine seaman, a good linguist, historian and ethnologist—a man of liberal culture and scientific tastes, interested in everything that tended to the improvement of the weapons and appliances of his profession.[1]

He was a fighter, too. While in the Mediterranean (1827–1829) he led a four-boat flotilla in the recapture of an English brig from a band of pirates. At the Washington Navy Yard he established the Depot of Charts and Instruments and again took leave—this time to fight the Seminoles. Promoted to commander in 1841, he commanded the *Ohio* in the attack on Tuxpan during the Mexican War, led a naval commission in the exploration of California and Oregon, and developed a friction primer to replace the old flintlock. During Stribling's superintendency, Goldsborough refused to pluck midshipmen from the school for his new Mediterranean command— a fact which, with his myriad other qualifications, seemed to make him a good choice for superintendent. Hence, he was ordered home from the Mediterranean to relieve Stribling. Crusty old commodores no longer robbed the Academy of its midshipmen. With the growing importance of Annapolis, it was the sea dog who was snatched.

Goldsborough was the St. Bernard of sea dogs. His 6 foot 4 inch frame and 300 pounds (one source says 400) made him look "tall as a sequoia and

---

¹Ford Manuscript, Ch. 14, p. 32.

Commander Louis M. Goldsborough. "Tall as a sequoia and as large as a mountain," the 6'4", 300-pound Goldsborough was both an intellectual and a fighter. Of all the antebellum superintendents, he best epitomized the Athens/Sparta mix that has long been the goal of Academy education. Courtesy: U.S. Naval Academy Archives

as large as a mountain."[2] A "superfluous" talker with a "piercing glance" and "brisk manner," he was

> a typical seaman of the old school; imposing in person, loud in voice, genial in temperament, and very much inclined to let the youngsters have their own way up to a certain limit, which, however, was fixed only in his mind. For the more sedate members of the Academic Board to come to him with complaints of the midshipmen's misbehavior, so long as he knew it was of the sort which always had been peculiar to midshipmen since they first began, rather nettled him, and he enjoyed giving the professor a reply savoring strongly of the brine, and which carried no satisfaction whatever. But let his limits be transgressed, and there was an uproar.[3]

Goldsborough's tolerant attitude toward discipline was likely the source of more than a few instances of fractious midshipmen behavior, especially toward the professors. But more than any other superintendent of the period, he reflected the free-wheeling spirit of the early Academy. More than that, he embodied those qualities that ennobled his profession—character, courage, patriotism, dedication, learning, and culture. Franklin Buchanan's title as the greatest of the antebellum superintendents is secure. But Louis M. Goldsborough may have been its most interesting personality.

Goldsborough's Crisis

> In this school is formed from the rough material the highly educated and most polished gentleman, to be put forth as a sample of his countrymen in any port and under any flag of Christendom.[4]

If this was Goldsborough's view of the Naval Academy and its midshipmen, he was soon disabused of the notion. For barely two weeks after taking office there occurred an incident that harkened back to the days of George Upshur. The actor in the drama was Midshipman Henry McThorne, whose conduct Goldsborough described to Secretary of the Navy James C. Dobbins:

> Mr. McThorne went beyond the limits of the Academy without my permission or authority, and while thus absent, he got shamefully drunk, & in this state entered the private dwelling-house of Mr. Alex Randall,

---

[2]Caspar Goodrich, "Memorabilia of the Old Navy," *U.S. Naval Institute Proceedings* 30 (December 1904): 823.

[3]Benjamin, *The United States Naval Academy*, p. 203.

[4]Stevens, *Annapolis*, p. 191, quoting a 26 March 1853 article entitled "The American Naval Academy" that appeared in the *Illustrated News*, a London magazine.

(a gentleman of this place of the highest respectability, & with whom, or whose family, Mr. McThorne had no acquaintance) ascended the stairway to the upper story unperceived by anyone of the numerous household . . . & there took off his clothes to his drawers, shirt & socks, & then dropped to sleep on the floor of a passage-way.

He was discovered in this situation by one of Mr. Randall's family & so remained until I on being notified of that fact by a message from that gentleman, caused an officer, accompanied by two servants, to go and bring him to his quarters. On his reaching here he was brought before me, & even at that time I found him to be still quite drunk, & otherwise in a disgusting condition.[5]

At Goldsborough's urging, Dobbins dismissed McThorne from the service. But the example was lost on the other midshipmen who seemed anxious to make their new superintendent's breaking-in period a trial by ordeal. Before his tour was up, Goldsborough's midshipmen had smoked, choked, insulted, assaulted, vandalized, pugilized, blazed, boozed, chewed, and cursed. Their exploits eventually evoked a warning from the president. In Chinese, the word crisis connotes both "danger" and "opportunity." Small men dwell on the danger. Goldsborough, no small man in any respect, seized the opportunity and used the crisis to win for the superintendent and the Academy some measure of the disciplinary power and independence that from the start should have been theirs.

"FOOL ME ONCE . . ."

The day after the McThorne report, Midshipman Livingston was suspended for "swearing, unofficerlike conduct on [the] parade ground, and treating [Professor] Lockwood with marked disrespect."[6] The next day, a pair of midshipmen were suspended for fighting—a week later two more, prompting Goldsborough to write to Secretary Dobbins of the midshipmen's "decided disposition for intemperance and other glaringly improper doings. . . ."[7] On 5 December, Midshipman Toon was reported for intoxication and within a week Midshipmen Garland and Maxwell were dismissed for the same reason. The very next day, 12 December, Midshipman Erben was discovered drunk in his room by Acting Master Edward Simpson. Erben's response of "Me, Sir?" to Simpson's accusation of drinking left

---

[5]Goldsborough to Dobbins, 14 November 1853, "Records of Naval Shore Establishments."

[6]*Journal of the Officer of the Day,* 15 November 1853.

[7]Goldsborough to Dobbins, 28 November 1853, "Records of Naval Shore Establishments."

no doubt as to his sobriety. According to Simpson, "His articulation and tones of voice verified the appearance of his face."[8]

The holidays brought a brief peace, but on New Year's Day 1854 Midshipman Campbell was suspended for making "improper noises" in his quarters and on 17 January Goldsborough informed Dobbins that four midshipmen had accumulated more than two hundred demerits and would be dropped from the rolls. Assigning demerits was one of the few disciplinary measures available to Goldsborough, but their effect on the midshipmen was not great and possibly counterproductive. One midshipman described demerits to his father:

> . . . a moderate lot of demerits don't do the least harm but show you are not quite subdued. As a general thing those who run a whole year without them are the outcasts of the institution who are friendless as well as spiritless.[9]

Rather than a deterrent, demerits were a badge of honor to the midshipmen. Goldsborough, too, saw their futility. Demerits were, he wrote,

> . . . a mere numerical register, as it were, in reference to violations of a certain sort, and carry with them a consequence at a final examination, and a more definite one in the event of amounting to a fixed number; but still they do not, and cannot, answer the purpose of punishing promptly and suitably an academic or military offense.[10]

Goldsborough had hit upon a fundamental weakness in the Academy's administration—the superintendent's lack of authority to mete out effective punishment to errant midshipmen. To restrain his young charges without such authority was like fighting the pirates without a cutlass.

Goldsborough was determined not to walk the plank. When on 28 February, Midshipman Brintnall invited Master Simpson to "kiss my ass," Goldsborough decided he had had enough. Writing to Secretary Dobbins on 2 March, he spoke of the midshipmen's propensity for hurling vulgarities from the safety of a group and then refusing to answer questions on the subject. The superintendent, he argued, should be empowered to answer such a silence with a Court of Inquiry.[11]

[8]Goldsborough to Dobbins, 12 December 1853, "Records of Naval Shore Establishments."

[9]Peter Karsten, *The Naval Aristocracy: The Golden Age of Annapolis and the Emergence of Modern American Navalism* (New York: The Free Press, 1972), p. 38.

[10]Ford Manuscript, Ch. 14, p. 5.

[11]Goldsborough to the Chief of the Bureau of Ordnance and Hydrography, 2 March 1854, "Records of Naval Shore Establishments."

On 4 March Goldsborough issued a general order of the superintendent. Officer instructors were put in charge of the midshipmen's dormitories to enforce regulations, observe marching to and from classes for "improprieties," and to check every room after taps. The New Revised Regulations of 1854 clamped down even more. Midshipmen were forbidden to land boats in town, to lounge on their beds during the day, to sit on the steps of halls and buildings, or to hang pictures or maps on the walls of their rooms without permission from the commandant. Beds were to be made and rooms cleaned prior to prayers at 7:15, barely a half hour after reveille. Except for the purser's office, dispensary, store, and officers' quarters during recreation hours, the midshipmen were forbidden to visit without the commandant's permission. The one exception was that they could visit with Goldsborough from noon to 2:00 P.M. without appointment or permission.[12]

Although the new regulations spawned a host of resignations, the situation improved, and by May Goldsborough was able to eliminate some of the midshipmen's demerits by reason of their good behavior. On 8 June, he recommended a leave of absence for the First Class because of their good conduct. Whether the new regulations or the onset of spring gave rise to this good behavior is not clear. But "Old Goldberry" had reason to hope that, with respect to the discipline problem, there was a glimmer of light at the end of the tunnel.

THE TOBACCO PROBLEM

Goldsborough's hopes were soon dashed, for on 14 June Midshipman Smith was caught puffing on a cigar and chewing tobacco. This fact, coupled with his intoxication and having previously broken into a professor's office, resulted in his resignation (to avoid dismissal). But the tobacco problem persisted at the school for many years. Chewing and cigars were viewed in the same light as boozing and bars—favorably by the midshipmen and with disgust by the school. George Dewey chewed tobacco and said, "It was the habit of the acting midshipmen in keeping with the universal male habit of the time."[13] One of the midshipmen's favorite songs of the 1850s contained the line, "Take your tobacco lively and pass the plug around."[14] Tobacco was used as a medium of exchange among the midshipmen—something to swap for, perhaps, a clean shirt so as to impress a lady friend.[15]

---

[12]*Journal of the Officer of the Day*, Introduction to 1854–57 Logbook.
[13]George Dewey, *Autobiography of George Dewey: Admiral of the Navy* (New York: Charles Scribner's Sons, 1913), p. 21.
[14]Puleston, *Annapolis*, p. 90.
[15]Ford Manuscript, Ch. 26, p. 17.

Academy officials saw tobacco as being at the root of many evils at the school. The 1860 Academic Board attributed the failure of a pair of midshipmen to their use of tobacco. An 1875 Navy Medical Board said of tobacco:

> . . . no doubt exists among medical men as to its injurious effects upon the growing organisms and mental powers of the young. Functional derangement of the digestive, circulatory, and nervous systems manifest themselves in the form of headache, confusion of intellect, loss of memory, impaired power of attention, lassitude, indisposition to muscular effort, nausea, want of appetite, dyspepsia, palpitation, tremulousness, disturbed sleep, impaired vision, etc., any one of which materially lessen the capacity for study and application. . . .
>
> The further evil of moral contamination from the necessarily unrestrained intercourse and language of the smoking room [is] superadded to physical and mental impairment.[16]

Every effort was made to discourage tobacco use, but suspensions and reprimands were inadequate, even when carried to an extreme. President Grant is said to have been reprimanded by an Academy guard for smoking a cigar while visiting the school. The "tobacco pledges" represented a different tack. Midshipmen who promised to avoid "the weed" would find themselves "freed" for town liberty or escorting privileges. As with the more famous "drinking pledges," the effect was only temporary. Midshipmen "passed the plug" for many years to come, and cigars no longer occasion remark. George Dewey gave up tobacco when he discovered that British officers did not chew. "I became convinced," explained Dewey, "that it was a filthy, vulgar habit in which no officer or gentleman should indulge."[17]

FROM SMOKING TO CHOKING

While the tobacco problem reflected the spirit of the times, there occurred on Christmas Day 1854 an incident that was hardly in the spirit of the season. One of the school's officers, Acting Master W. K. Mayo, was seized and choked by a midshipman. The outraged Mayo reported the affair to Goldsborough:

---

[16]E. M. Eller, "Report: The Use of Tobacco by the Cadets at the U.S. Naval Academy," *U.S. Naval Institute Proceedings* 95 (December 1969): 153.

[17]Dewey, *Autobiography*, p. 21. The comment reveals more about the naval officer's mind than it relates to tobacco.

U.S. Naval Academy
Dec. 27, 1854

Sir.

I deem it my duty to make the following report, viz.

As I was returning to my room between the hours of ten P.M. and Midnight of the 25 inst, I observed a number of persons enter building No. 3, in which are my quarters. I entered it—but a very few moments after them. The passage was pitchy dark . . . .

As I entered the lower door, I heard the sound of feet on the second floor, as if some persons were coming to a halt near the head of the upper flight of steps. As I ascended the first flight, with my left hand upon the bannister as a guide, I saw distinctly . . . a person descending, who seemed to take the bannister also as a guide. The general appearance of this person, induced in me the belief that, he was one of the occupants of the building who was going out necessarily, and I carefully turned to the right . . . yielding to him the bannister. I had gotten upon the platform, when, much to my astonishment, I felt the pressure of two hands, fairly and deliberately put about my throat. I thought then that the person who thus assailed me, was excited by the Spirit of the holy-day times, and in frolicking humor, had taken me for one of his companions, and I asked him, if he were not mistaken? To this, I received no other reply, than the tightening of the grasp about my throat. Still unable to believe that an officer of the U.S. Navy, could by any principle, assail a brother officer . . . I peremptorily demanded of the assailant if he knew whom he had hold of? To this I received no reply.[18]

It took the "full strength" of a nearby midshipman to pry the hands of the perpetrator, Midshipman Walker, from Mayo's neck. Walker was dismissed from the service, but he was surely not the last midshipman to feel animus toward the Academy's Executive Department. In contrast to the early days of the school when officers and midshipmen were regarded with some sense of equality, the new organization cast them in the roles of superior and subordinate. The Executive Department thus became, and remains, a kind of police force with the result that midshipmen have tended to view many of the Academy's officers as adversaries rather than as role models.[19] Alfred Thayer Mahan alluded to this feeling which in the 1850s was just beginning to develop:

A general good-humored tolerance . . . characterized the relations of the officers and students. Primarily, each were in the appreciation of the others

---

[18]Mayo to Goldsborough, 27 December 1854, "Records of the Naval Academy."
[19]Samuel R. Franklin switched from the Academy's Executive Department to the Department of Ethics and English studies because he disliked the "espionage" expected of him.

A round house not the enemy's
A traitor's fate shall earn.
And if a man there be
Who does this traitor know
And keeps it to himself, the same
Shall suffer death also.

The vile incendiary
I fear is midst you now
And if you don't expose him
He will get you in a row.
I too have been at school
And then it was my way
To tell of my companions
As you should do today.

Once more and last I say
I do admonish all
Who know one bit of this foul deed
Out of the ranks to fall.
What! no one speaks! Ye Gods!
And can't the man be found,
Who burnt down (Sir Adjutant)
Our Round House to the ground.

Chorus:

It is well then to tell then
Who did this "grievous ill"
And damn him, I'll hang him
So help me Bob I will.[25]

In the end, no one was hanged or court-martialed. But the uproar in Annapolis had caught the attention of President Pierce, who urged that the "most rigorous and summary measures" be adopted to "suppress the vice of intemperance at the Naval Academy."[26] The involvement of the president in the daily disciplinary affairs of the school argued strongly for increasing the authority of the superintendent. Already, Goldsborough had put the case convincingly to Commodore Charles Morris, chief of the Bureau of Ordnance and Hydrography:

> As things now stand, the Superintendent is rather a mere medium of complaints than an officer possessed of distinct authority to redress constantly occurring wrongs, which fact operates against his military influence

[25]Ford Manuscript, Ch. 14, pp. 25, 34–35.
[26]Acting Secretary of the Navy Charles W. Welsh to Goldsborough, 21 April 1855, "Records of the Naval Academy."

and, what is of still greater consequence, against the general welfare of the Academy. Of all things too, his authority should not be wanting, as it is, in the particular of ascertaining, with certainty, the perpetrators of grave offenses. He may, it is true, proceed to inquiries and even admonish all collectively; but neither nor both combined is likely to prove effectual, simply because they cannot reach the real delinquents with any kind of certainty . . . .

At West Point, the Superintendent is empowered to inflict punishments of various classes, and to institute garrison, or regimental courts-martial, at which, by causing testimony to be taken under oath, he can reach an offender against the regulations with almost infallible certainty. Our system must be made equally stringent, if it be desired that this establishment should attain a really proud degree of excellence.[27]

Commodore Morris concurred and urged Goldsborough to develop a system of punishments. Goldsborough did so and Dobbins instituted it.

"Punishments by the Superintendent"

1st Class - Confinement to the limits of the Academic grounds
           Private reprimands
           Deprivation of recreation within the grounds
           Confinement to room
           Reprimand to be read on parade
           Suspension from recitations, drills and exercises
2nd Class - Confinement in guard room

"Punishments by the Secretary of the Navy"

3rd Class - Dismissal, unless the offender avail himself of a privilege that
           may be granted to him of resigning
           Public Dismissal

Although it did not provide for a West Point-style inquiry, the new system gave the superintendent real disciplinary clout. Goldsborough and his successors were free to confine, reprimand, suspend, and—in effect—incarcerate those who strayed from the straight and narrow. Midshipmen who refused to submit to the new punishments faced dismissal. The old "gentleman midshipman" was giving way to a new breed—still spirited, still proud, but increasingly subordinate. This transformation was a major development of the Goldsborough era and was a prerequisite to the Academy's growing independence. If Annapolis was to be the repository and inculcator of the ideals and professional standards of the service, it had to gain control of its midshipmen.

---

[27]Ford Manuscript, Ch. 14, pp. 5–6.

Academics and Professional Training

Goldsborough also put his stamp on the Academy's academic and professional program, but to a lesser degree than in the disciplinary area. This was due to several factors. First, the major curricular and organizational reforms had occurred under Stribling, leaving Goldsborough the task of administering and fine-tuning them. Second, action in the academic area involved the Academic Board with whom credit for any progress must be shared. Third, the romance and antiintellectualism of the old sailing navy was still felt. Finally, the Academy itself had not yet settled on a coherent philosophy of education.

ACADEMICS—"A DAMNED SIGHT TOO MUCH SCIENCE"?

An officer should be "capable of performing any duty, practical or scientific." So said the Academic Board in a 17 June 1853 letter. The academic program for 1854—the first year in which there were four classes—reflected this practical and scientific bent, as can be seen in Table 5-1.[28]

Goldsborough's acquisition of additional astronomical and scientific equipment for the school, and his attempts to improve the curriculum and raise standards, evoked from navy conservatives the complaint that he was introducing "a damned sight too much science into the institution."[29] That comment, however, must be viewed in light of the conservatives' opposition to scientific training in general. Many felt that the school's program was too practical. In fact, Park Benjamin suggests that "intellectual indigestion" was at the root of the school's drinking problem.[30]

Be that as it may, intellect was coming to count for more than personal courage in the making of naval officers. The Merit Rolls ensured this. Based on course grades and conduct, the Merit Rolls determined order of rank in the service. Midshipmen who did not excel in their studies

> had the mortification of seeing their more studious classmates in the enjoyment of rank which the slow process of promotion by seniority and the uncertain tenure of life might prevent them from ever reaching. A difference of ten numbers in a graduating class often proved to be an impassable gulf separating a Lieutenant from the honors and responsibilities of command forever.[31]

Avoidance of "mortification" proved powerful incentive and midshipmen performance improved throughout Goldsborough's tour. Whereas the fail-

[28]Minutes of the Academic Board, "Records of the Naval Academy."
[29]Sweetman, *The U.S. Naval Academy*, p. 46.
[30]Quoted in Karsten, *The Naval Aristocracy*, p. 48.
[31]Ford Manuscript, Ch. 14, pp. 7–8.

Table 5-1. The 1854 Academic Program

Department	Session	Days Received	Subjects and Books
First Class Year			
Seamanship and	1	M W F 1	
tactics	2	T 2	
Astronomy and	1	M T Th F 1	Practical astronomy
navigation	2	T 1 Th 1, 2, 3	Optics
			Theory of navigational
			surveying
Natural and	1	M W F 3	Laroner on heat, electricity
experimental philosophy	2	M W F 3	Maine & Brown on the
			marine steam engine
			Inorganic chemistry
Gunnery and	1	W - Sat 1	Page's *Theorie du pointage*
infantry tactics	2	T 3 Sat 1	Mordecai on gunpowder
			Knowlton's *Notes on*
			Gunpowder
Ethics and	1	T Th 3	Wayland's *Moral Science*
English studies	2	M W F 2	Kent's *Constitutional and*
			International Law
Spanish	1	M - F	Ollendorff's *Methods*
Second Class Year			
Natural and	1	M - F 2	Bartlett's *Mechanics of Solids*
experimental	2	M W F 2	Bartlett's *Mechanics of*
philosophy			*Liquids*
			Bartlett's *Mechanics of*
			Fluids
Gunnery and	1	Sat 1	Small arms, field, artillery,
infantry tactics	2	Sat 1	etc. Dahlgren's *Boat*
			Armament.
Ethics and	2	T Th 2	Newman's *Rhetoric*
English studies			
French	1	M - F 3	Manesca's *French Reader*
Spanish	2	M W F 3	Ollendorff's *Methods*
Drawing	1	T Th	Use of water colors
Third Class Year			
Mathematics	1	M - Sat 1	Davies's *Legendre's Geometry*
	2	M - Sat 1	Chauvenet's *Trigonometry*
			Davies's *Mensuration*
			Davies's *Descriptive Geometry*
Ethics and	1	T Th 2	Worcester & Lord's history
English studies	2	T Th 2	Lord's history of the U.S.
			Composition

out the special purposes for which the Academy is supported."[39] Still, Goldsborough received an annual library appropriation of $2,000 from Congress, along with the privilege of importing foreign books duty-free through the Treasury Department.[40]

The classification and numbers of books acquired during the 1856–57 academic year reveal quite a shift from the earlier nautical emphasis:

Scientific	218 volumes
Nautical	66
Documentary and historical	334
Travels and geography	62
Literary and miscellaneous	320
	1000 volumes[41]

These figures are from a June 1857 report by Assistant Librarian Thomas G. Ford. Ford also had figures on library use:

Volumes drawn by midshipmen	2950
by officers	1100
	4050

Since the library by this time contained some 6,725 volumes, the use rate was high, even assuming that the 4,050 figure included many books drawn several times over. Ford should have been pleased with the library's evident success. But he was not:

> I have noticed that the members of the Fourth Class have been the most constant visitors to the library and have drawn more books therefrom, in proportion, than the members of the higher classes. The most extensive readers in this class, however, are to be found in the lowest sections of the same . . . . Among the members of the Third Class there is an evident leaning toward a higher class of reading—history, for instance . . . but they rarely read works on history from beginning to end—one or two volumes are glanced over, the matter proves dry, or uninteresting, and the wearied mind takes refuge in a novel or periodical . . . . The members of the Second Class are more addicted to the reading of history, and of serious works, in general, than those below them. They begin to manifest a desire to know something of the world by their demand for books of travel. They also give to the Poets and Literati a fair share of attention. Scientific works are sometimes consulted in reference to the subject-matter of their studies . . . . The reading of the First Class is of a miscellaneous character, but, chiefly, serious and instructive. They have already read the lighter class of works, and are compelled, either from taste or necessity, to fall back upon

[39]Chief of the Bureau of Ordnance and Hydrography to Goldsborough, "Records of the Naval Academy."
[40]Ford Manuscript, Ch. 14, p. 16.
[41]Ford to Chauvenet, 13 June 1857, "Records of the Naval Academy."

books which they neglected hitherto . . . . Each student is allowed to draw two volumes, weekly, from the library, and many of them borrow, in addition, the books of their classmates; and it is evident that all this reading cannot be accomplished without large inroads into the hours allotted to study . . . . In a word, the library, under the present system, is not productive—to the students—of half the good of which it is capable. Classical literature, and, I am sorry to say it, American history are left in comparative neglect, and our choice collection of French works is hardly even touched.[42]

The next year Ford wrote a similar letter to the new superintendent, Captain George S. Blake, and another in 1859 in which he referred to "the laggards [who] read all the books they are permitted to take from the library, and as many more as they can get hold of."[43] Although his zeal in this matter is puzzling, Ford was likely correct in maintaining that the library was a diversion for the unstudious. His views must have carried some weight, for midshipmen of the Fourth Class were restricted in their use of the library during the academic year 1858–59.[44] The 1859 Board of Visitors urged that the restrictions extend to the upper classes as well. As if to preserve their intellectual interests, a group of midshipmen had recently organized the Lawrence Literary Society—one of the school's first legitimate extracurricular activities. All of this may bear on the surprising number of naval officers who dabbled in writing of all kinds in the decades following the Civil War.

Faculty Affairs

By the mid-1850s, a decade of development had produced a faculty that was beginning to take modern form. Including Goldsborough, the staff of the Academy numbered twenty-four for the 1853–54 year. It included "some of the brightest minds in the service."[45] Officers on the academic staff included the commandant, assistant commandant (Samuel Marcy of the original 1845 staff), and four acting masters who were assistant professors and recent graduates of the school (Edward Simpson of the Spirits Club was one). The other twelve on the academic staff were the "civilian" professors of whom Chauvenet, Lockwood, and Girault were veterans of the 1845 days. Also on staff were a surgeon, purser, chaplain, secretary, and a clerk.

---

[42]Ibid.

[43]Ford to Blake, 9 July 1859, "Records of the Naval Academy."

[44]By Ford's own accounting, the results were dramatic. The number of books checked out of the library by all classes dropped from 4,000 during 1857–58 to 3,147 during 1858–59; with the Fourth Class the drop was from 2,432 to 600.

[45]Ford Manuscript, Ch. 14, p. 1.

The faculty was structured much as it is today and had some of the same problems. Professional training and discipline were under the commandant; academics were the prerogative of the Academic Board which was dominated by Professor Chauvenet, whose "clear perceptions and good judgement [enabled] him on all occasions to say and do the right thing."[46] The civilian professors were becoming less navylike, thanks to an 1852 change in regulations which no longer required them to wear an officer's uniform.[47] Even in civilian dress, though, the professors—by way of superior education and longevity at the school—enjoyed a measure of ascendancy over the junior officer instructors. The 1854 and 1855 Boards of Visitors recommended longer tours of duty for the officers; the 1857 Board urged that they be chosen from the ranks of the navy rather than from the new graduates of the school. Still, many of the officers were excellent instructors. Several taught from their own manuscripts and had authored treatises on professional subjects. Lieutenant Billy Parker, assistant professor of mathematics, was said to be second only to Chauvenet as a teacher while at the school.

Goldsborough did what he could to improve the lot of his staff. To promote "harmony and contentment" among the bachelor officers and assistant professors, he set aside a room in the Mess Hall building and furnished it for their use as a messroom and lounge.[48] For the benefit of all instructors he issued the following rule:

> Barring misapprehensions and mistakes, a Professor's opinion as to the class-mark a student should receive, must necessarily be conclusive; nor can I ever permit the opinion of the student, even when backed by every member of his class to have a countervailing influence.[49]

On the issue of pay, however, Goldsborough was able to do little. In 1852, Professors Lockwood and Hopkins had requested that Annapolis professors be paid on the same footing as those at West Point, but to no avail. Hopkins renewed the argument in 1853, pointing out that a professor on the Hudson received nearly $3,000 in pay and benefits a year. The

---

[46]Ibid., p. 33. According to Ford, Chauvenet "was undoubtedly the ablest and most satisfying instructor the Academy ever had—the most brilliant mind—the best thinker—far ahead of his time."

[47]Instead of a uniform, they wore "navy blue cloth, citizen's dress-coats, for full dress, and navy blue frock-coats, for undress, both with navy buttons; and plain white, or navy blue vests and pantaloons, with round black hats. No swords." Kennedy to Stribling, 13 August 1852, "Records of the Naval Academy."

[48]At the same time, he kept his officers under tight rein. When Lieutenant Scott ignored the prohibition against drinking and smoking in his room, Goldsborough initiated court-martial proceedings. Scott backed down.

[49]Ford Manuscript, Ch. 14, p. 23.

same professor was paid $1,500 on the Severn.[50] These views were endorsed by the 1854 Board of Examiners, but this and subsequent recommendations in 1855 and 1856 went unheeded in Washington.[51] For years the Academy's professors continued to provide services far more valuable to the navy than the remuneration they received in return.

Austerity Hits Annapolis

The professors failed to fatten their wallets because Congress was tightening its belt—and with it, the Academy's purse strings. Of the $53,678 requested for the 1854–55 fiscal year, less than $40,000 was appropriated. Goldsborough was directed to limit expenditures to these items:[52]

1st - complete gas works and expand to officer quarters and lamp posts	$3,000
2nd - fuel for heating and lighting	4,000
3rd - continuing seawall and levelling and filling in grounds	10,000
4th - new gate at Guard House	3,525
5th - workshop for engine repair	1,150
6th - tools for engine repair	1,350
7th - repairs of buildings	3,000
8th - furniture and fixtures	3,000
9th - books	2,000
10th - stationery	500
11th - electric clock	200
12th - theodolite	275
13th - incidentals	1,500
14th - watchmen, laborers, assistants, attendants	6,368

Appropriations for the next three years totaled $48,044.22, $39,595.22, and $42,307.22 respectively. In each of those years, as in 1854–55, the upkeep and expansion of the Academy's physical plant received highest priority. The chapel and observatory begun under Stribling were completed in 1854. Of the 1855–56 budget ($48,044.22),

---

[50]Estimated pay for the Academy's staff for the 1854–55 year is as follows: superintendent and executive officer, twenty-five hundred dollars; assistant to executive officer (a lieutenant), fifteen hundred dollars; professors, fifteen hundred dollars; assistant professors, one thousand dollars.

[51]"Records of the Naval Academy."

[52]Chief of the Bureau of Ordnance and Hydrography to Goldsborough, 16 August 1854, "Records of the Naval Academy."

Midshipman John G. Walker, shown here in standard midshipman dress uniform as prescribed by the 1853 regulations. His sword is of the 1841 regulation pattern. Courtesy: U.S. Naval Institute Collection

Attendant at gas and heat apparatus	638.75
Attendant at gas and heat apparatus	456.25
Laborers to attend midshipmen	
quarters and grounds	1,640.00
	$7,360.22[62]

The Academy's building program provided further infusions of money and jobs for the local economy, not to mention the payroll of the midshipmen and staff. Even in years of low funding, federal dollars to the Academy in the form of wages and other appropriations totaled upward of $100,000, much of which found its way into the Annapolis economy.

Letters to the superintendent seeking jobs were numerous, the openings few. Upshur once received a letter signed by twenty-four men attesting to what a good painter and glazier the applicant was. Annapolis politicians sometimes tried to influence hiring. Goldsborough once complained of this to the secretary, saying that he seldom went into town, never mixed with politicians, and hired only on the basis of ability—not politics or religion. Being a sea dog with a shore command had its drawbacks.

Making Room for Annapolis

For Goldsborough, the privilege of presiding over the Academy's first graduation under the four-year program on 10 June 1854 likely provided some consolation for the unpleasantries of jobbery. Six of the ten midshipmen in the advanced class formed in 1851 had completed the accelerated course to become the first real "graduates" of the Naval Academy. Thomas O. Selfridge was number one in his class, followed by John Cain, Joseph N. Miller, Henry D. Todd, John S. Barnes (of outhouse fame), and John M. Stribling.[63]

The ceremony was simple. Students, faculty, and the Board of Examiners mustered in the Chapel at noon. The chaplain offered prayers, Goldsborough made a brief speech, and the certificates of graduation were presented. The parchment certificate was ornamented by a blue ribbon and a representation of the practice ship *Preble*, and was signed by the Board of Examiners. It read:

[62]Chief of the Bureau of Ordnance and Hydrography to Goldsborough, 13 April 1855, "Records of the Naval Academy."

[63]Selfridge, Miller, and Barnes all taught at the Naval Academy and had distinguished Civil War careers. Miller became known as "Ironclad Joe" from his service on monitors. Barnes left the service in 1869 after publishing a treatise on "Submarine Warfare: Offensive and Defensive." He became a merchant in New York. Selfridge became a rear admiral and lived until 1924.

United States Naval Academy,
Annapolis, Maryland.

We, the Academic Board, having thoroughly examined Acting Midshipman_____on all the subjects, theoretical and practical, taught at conformity with the Regulations, grant him this Certificate of Graduation, and recommend him to the President of the United States for the appointment of Midshipman in the Naval Service.

In Witness whereof, we, severally, subscribe our names hereunto, this _____day of_____in the year of our Lord _____, and of the Independence of the United Sates the _____.[64]

Events were at work to open positions for these new graduates. In 1855 Congress passed the Naval Efficiency Act which aimed at a system of promotion by merit instead of by longevity.[65] The 1855 act created a "Naval Retiring Board of Fifteen" which, after reviewing some 712 officers, found 201 to be "incapable of performing promptly and efficiently all their duty both ashore and afloat."[66] They were retired or stricken from the rolls. This "Star Chamber Board," as it was referred to by its victims, included former Superintendents Stribling and Buchanan, Captain Matthew C. Perry, and several other senior officers who had been on the various Boards of Examiners that visited the Academy. The act won the "hearty support" of Goldsborough and the Academy's officers, for it encouraged diligence among the midshipmen "who could now look forward to promotion to the grade of Lieutenant before losing their useful vigor and inclination for the service."[67] The axe had fallen and had rooted out the navy's dead wood. Annapolites would soon have their day in the sun.

Men of Annapolis

In April 1856, a symbol of the new navy, the recently completed steam frigate *Merrimac*, visited Annapolis. President Franklin Pierce used the occasion to visit the Academy which honored him with a twenty-one-gun salute and a naval ball. The Pierce administration aimed at reviving the navy from the doldrums of the past several decades.

---

[64]Ford Manuscript, Ch. 14, p. 13.

[65]Of 68 captains in the service in 1854, the youngest was fifty-six. Seventy-four of the 97 commanders were between fifty and fifty-five. The 327 lieutenants ranged from thirty to fifty, the 198 passed midshipmen from twenty-one to thirty-seven years. One captain had been unemployed for thirty-six of his fifty-four years of service. Another had spent only two of his thirty service years at sea. One commander in 1848 had not been to sea for more than forty-one years. Paullin, *Paullin's History*, pp. 239–40.

[66]Ford Manuscript, Ch. 14, p. 30.

[67]Ibid., p. 31. Goldborough was promoted to captain as a result of the 1855 Act.

With its combination of sail and steam power, the *Merrimac* itself symbolized a navy in transition. Its visit to the Academy was symbolic in another way, too. Acting almost as if on cue, three Old Navy commodores had recently passed away.[68] The Civil War would finally mark an end to the romantic tradition of the old frigate navy in which physical courage, individual daring, and the willingness to shed blood at the slightest affront to national honor counted so much. The two most famous 1850s graduates of the Naval Academy were George Dewey and Alfred Thayer Mahan, naval officers of a much different mold from the Joneses, Truxtons, and Decaturs of the past. The age of the commodores had faded. The men of Annapolis were now at the helm.

[68]Commodores Morris, Conner, and McKeever.

CHAPTER SIX
OFFICERS AND GENTLEMEN:
THE ANNAPOLIS IDEAL

It is by no means enough that an officer of the Navy should be a capable mariner. He must be that, of course, but also a great deal more. He should be as well a gentleman of liberal education, refined manners, punctilious courtesy, and the nicest sense of personal honor.

—a definition based on the words of John Paul Jones

Ask any new plebe at the Naval Academy, "What is a naval officer?", and you will likely get a perfect rendition of the above. In fact, it is only one of a host of definitions, quotations, and sayings memorized and spat out in knee-jerk fashion by new midshipmen as part of their introduction to Academy life. Most are nonsensical, such as the alliterative response to the question, "Why didn't you say sir?":

> Sir, sir is a subservient word surviving from the surly days in Old Serbia, when certain serfs, too ignorant to remember their lords' names, yet too servile to blaspheme them, circumvented the situation by serogating the subservient word, sir, by which I now belatedly address a certain senior cirruped who correctly surmised that I am syrupy enough to say sir after every word I said, sir![1]

But the words of John Paul Jones are not nonsense. To the contrary, they connote what might be called the Annapolis ideal—the idea that, by virtue of his selection as an officer candidate, his unique Academy training, and his life of service to the country, the Annapolis man is someone special— someone like John Paul Jones. Jones was a man not only of great physical courage and daring, as shown in the epic encounter with *Serapis*, but a man whose "refinement" graced European society, a man whose sense of courtesy and personal honor shone in his conduct during and after the 1778 raid on

---

[1] From *Reef Points*, a handbook of naval information and trivia issued to all new midshipmen.

St. Mary's Isle in Scotland,[2] and a man whose views on liberal education made him one of the first proponents of a Naval Academy. It is for good reason that Jones is considered the Father of the American Navy. The fact that his body was dug up in Paris and interred in 1905 in the Naval Academy's chapel-mausoleum (perhaps the most sacred place in the Yard), enhanced Jones's stature. Small wonder that at Annapolis, when John Paul Jones talks—people listen.[3]

Midshipman Alfred Miles likely had an ear to the Jones legend when in 1907 he wrote the Academy's alma mater, "Anchors Aweigh," of which the last two lines are:

> Faith, Courage, Service true
> With honor over, honor over all.

Education, manners, courtesy, honor, faith, courage, and service—all of these are part of the Annapolis ideal. But ideals and values are not easily inculcated. If there was an inculation process, or an "Annapolis stamp" as it has been put, it can only be understood by examining the total Academy experience—from the classroom to the ballroom, from appointment to graduation. Although the chapters that preceded this one alighted on some of these subjects, our sketch thus far of the Old Naval Academy is mostly a skeleton. It is time to bring these bones to life.

The Raw Material: Who Came and Why

> Both those entering the officer corps and those reaching its highest ranks in the years after the Civil War were a cross section of middle class America.
>
> Samuel Huntington

> Samuel Huntington has claimed that cadets and midshipmen of the nineteenth century were "a cross section of middle class America," a "mirror of the nation." These statements require considerable qualification.
>
> Peter Karsten

Easily the most provocative study of the Naval Academy and the officer corps it produced is Peter Karsten's *The Naval Aristocracy: the Golden Age of Annapolis and the Emergence of Modern American Navalism, 1845–1925.*

---

[2]Jones and his men went ashore to kidnap the earl of Selkirk. Upon finding that the earl was not there, Jones returned to his ship, but his men stayed behind long enough to steal the earl's silver. Upon discovering this, Jones purchased the silver from his men using his own funds and returned it to the earl.

[3]Midshipman John Stone held Jones's hand during the autopsy in 1905. This writer met Mr. Stone in 1977 and shook the hand of a man who "shook the hand" of John Paul Jones.

Karsten's thesis is that during Annapolis's "golden age" there existed a composite, model naval officer whose upper-class origins, Academy indoctrination, and isolation from civilian society made him—and the officer corps he represented—elitist, inbred, narrow, and excessively dedicated to the ideals of the service. So intense was this identification with service, argues Karsten, that officers placed the navy's interest above that of the nation. In Karsten's view, the Naval Academy began a life-long process of professional socialization that resulted in officers who publicly advocated an ever-larger navy not as a means to an end, that is, national defense, but as an end in itself; not as a force for peace but as a vehicle to gain glory for service and self in war. Thus, the navalism that had its birth in 1845 was linked to the Vietnam War.

Like all seminal works, Karsten's has been criticized—about which more later. But on the issue of the social origins of the midshipmen, he is on target. As noted in the first chapter, midshipmen appointments had long been influenced by national and naval politics—a fact evidenced by great naval clans like the Rodgers and the Perrys, and by actions like John Quincy Adams's appointment of fifty new midshipmen in February 1829 so as to cheat (as democrats viewed it) Andrew Jackson from the spoils of victory. In fact, the birth of the Naval Academy can be linked, via the *Somers* mutiny, to the politicized appointment process. Midshipman Philip Spencer, it will be recalled, was the son of the secretary of war.

The establishment of the Academy and the system of congressional appointment of midshipmen further politicized the process. "Appointments were due entirely to the political favor of representatives in Congress," wrote George Dewey of the 1850s.[4] Thomas G. Ford lamented that poor but able youths were passed over in favor of those with family and party connections. Sometimes money helped, as shown by a congressman in 1873 being paid $1,700 by a man hoping to get his stepson appointed. As Karsten notes, "Political patronage was absolutely essential to a young man who hoped to embark on a career as an officer in Uncle Sam's Navy."[5] What he fails to mention is that this was more a negative reflection on Congress than on the Naval Academy or the navy.

The Academy's problem was that it still lacked the institutional strength necessary for the wholesale rejection of unfit appointees. The entrance exam was cursory at best. Of 1,522 candidates nominated and appointed between 1851 and 1863, 1,209 were admitted.[6] An 1857 report by the comman-

---

[4]Dewey, *Autobiography*, p. 12.
[5]Karsten, *The Naval Aristocracy*, p. 6.
[6]By way of comparison, between 1934 and 1947 there were 43,547 applicants, 8,358 of whom were admitted and 6,232 of whom graduated. Walter C. Ford and J. Buroughs Stokes, "The Selection and Procurement of Better Candidate Material For the Naval Academy," *U.S. Naval Institute Proceedings* 72 (April 1946): 22.

dant of midshipmen spoke of the need for a better entrance exam, but cited the danger of a public institution having standards that were too tight. Ability rather than knowledge should be emphasized, said the report. According to Robley Evans, it was well that the entrance exam was simple, "otherwise many of us would not have followed the Navy as a career."[7] Since of the 1,209 midshipmen admitted between 1851 and 1863 only 209 graduated, a loose entrance exam merely postponed the inevitable for many. Thus, if the Academy engendered a politicized congressional appointment system, it also provided a means for ferreting out the unfit. Rather than six out of seven, the attrition rate today is about one of three.

Congressional appointments also ensured an officer corps that was more geographically representative of the nation. Whereas "over 80 percent of the midshipmen appointed before 1860 came from one of the original 13 colonies, by 1866 43 percent were from the Middle Atlantic states, 25 percent from New England, 26 percent from Midwestern states and only 5 percent from the South."[8] Robley Evans described the 127 men in his class as "an average lot from all parts of the country, and representing the various classes of American life."[9] New England might continue to dominate the merchant fleet. But on men-of-war, all sections counted.

Although all classes of American life were represented in his class, Robley Evans's class was not *representative* of all classes of American life. A perusal of the Academy's Register of Candidates for the 1847–60 period illustrates this. The register lists all midshipmen candidates from 1847 to 1860, noting their age, hometown, state, father's occupation, and whether they graduated. I have identified all or part of this information on 369 graduates, 368 nongraduates, and 152 appointees who were rejected at the preliminary examination by the Academic Board or by the Medical Board. Table 6-1 shows my findings.[10]

Clearly, Annapolites did not mirror the nation at large. Over 66 percent of all candidates came from backgrounds that represented less than 5 percent of the population (officers, lawyers, government officials, doctors, including druggists and civil engineers, and merchants). Whereas agriculture was the livelihood of over half of all Americans, only about one in every six or seven candidates came from this background. Thirty percent of all candidates lived in cities of greater than 100,000 population compared with only 10 percent of the general population. Nearly one half had

[7]Robley D. Evans, *A Sailor's Log: Recollections of a Naval Life* (New York: D. Appleton, 1901), p. 35. One applicant in 1859 failed the entrance exam because of "timidity."

[8]Karsten, *The Naval Aristocracy*, p. 5. By 1896, the figures were Middle Atlantic, 32 percent; New England, 10 percent; West, 36 percent; Old South, 22 percent.

[9]Evans, *A Sailor's Log*, p. 36.

[10]"Records of the Naval Academy."

Table 6–1. Social Origins of the Midshipmen (percentage)

Father's Occupation	Country at Large 1870*	Appointees	Rejected Ac. Bd.	Graduated	Nongraduated
Officer	0.03	14.4	1	12.4	6.5
Agriculture	51.00	15.9	31	13.3	18.2
Banker	0.15	1.7	–	1.6	1.7
Lawyer	0.50	15.0	12	14.4	15.4
Manufacturer	0.50	1.3	–	1.2	1.4
Gov't. Off.	0.60	7.8	5	9.2	6.5
Doctors, Druggists, Civil Eng.	1.10	13.3	13	13.7	13.0
Merchants	2.50	15.9	12	16.4	15.4
Clergy, Teachers, Artists	1.10	1.8	2	2.0	2.7
Shopkeeper, Agent, Hotelkeeper	2.00	7.6	5	8.4	6.8
Artisan, Clerk	40.20	10	20	7.2	12.3

*Source: Karsten, *The Naval Aristocracy, p. 9, based on data drawn from the 1870 census.*

attended private schools before entering the Academy. Those who did not, presumably of a lower socioeconomic group, were at a disadvantage as shown by the high number of rejections by the Academic Board among those of an agricultural background. Thus, Karsten is correct in his conclusion that "commercial, manufacturing and professional classes were overrepresented at Annapolis, and that the agricultural interests and the working classes were underrepresented."[11]

Political clout and educational advantage were two reasons the sons of businessmen, doctors, lawyers, and officers were so numerous at Annapolis. These points go to the issue of why Annapolis (or rather their congressmen) chose them. But why did these young men choose Annapolis? According to Thomas G. Ford, the Academy's attraction was that it offered a professional education, increasing pay and rank, and chances for distinction and glory. Peter Karsten cites family pressure (in the case of officers' sons), militarism, the "lure of the bounding main and a gold-braided sleeve," and the residue of naval glory from the War of 1812 that survived in books like James

[11]Karsten, *The Naval Aristocracy,* p. 8.

Fenimore Cooper's *Lives of Distinguished American Naval Officers* and *Naval History of the United States* and in a whole genre of naval literature that glorified midshipman life in the same way as did the 1950s television show, "Men of Annapolis."[12]

If the legends and literature of frigate victories past were part of the allure of Annapolis, so too may it have benefitted from the romance of the clippership era. For a brief period during the 1850s, the volume of trade carried under the Stars and Stripes was greater than that hauled by the Union Jack. The majesty of billowing canvas and tall ships undoubtedly influenced many appointees, especially in eastern ports. Perhaps the chances of a young lad in rural areas west of the Appalachians to be similarly aroused were not as great. For many Americans the frontier began just beyond the last tree they had felled. That these folks did not send their sons to Annapolis should not be surprising. Midshipmen who did come from less privileged backgrounds may have seen the Academy as a vehicle for upward mobility. And for candidates of all social classes, patriotism surely played a role in donning the uniform. It is impossible to identify any single factor as the most important one in choosing Annapolis. If there were a composite model naval officer in this period, his reasons for entering the profession would be varied.

What They Found: The Annapolis Experience

SOCIETY AND CULTURE

The midshipman candidates who made their way to Annapolis found a city whose commercial glory had passed but whose "traditional intelligence remained."[13] Refinement, hospitality, and good cheer characterized Annapolis society in colonial times, and according to Samuel R. Franklin it was still "very pleasant" in the 1850s.[14] The Academy had played a role in this by sparing Annapolis "the humiliation of sinking into poverty on the one hand, or being vulgarized and exploited as an industrial town on the other."[15] The Academy's infusion of revenue into the local economy has already been mentioned, but other factors were equally important. Professor Girault, for example, helped found a new church in Annapolis. Many of the Academy's faculty became prominent in civic affairs. In later years,

---

[12]Alfred Vagts argues that "militarism with its glamour and hard service scarcely got a hold in American imagination until after the opening of the twentieth century." Alfred A. Vagts, *A History of Militarism: Civilian and Military*, rev. ed. (New York: Meridian Books, 1959), p. 103.

[13]Riley, *The Ancient City*, p. 274.

[14]Franklin, *Memoirs*, p. 144.

[15]Stevens, *Annapolis*, p. 327.

retired naval officers would make their mark on the town. So, too, did the Academy's presence, like St. John's College, serve to enhance the intellectual climate of Annapolis. Although St. John's and the Naval Academy have come to represent quite different educational traditions, their prestige has benefitted Annapolis.

The Academy and Annapolis provided each other a measure of social variety. Marylander Franklin Buchanan and his wife put the school's relations with the town on the right track from the start, and it was not long before the best families in Annapolis received the midshipmen into their homes. Balls, circuses, fairs, and St. John's commencements were all attended by the midshipmen, not to mention a few taverns and pool halls. The section of Annapolis known as Hell Point just outside of the Academy's number one gate was notorious for this latter type of entertainment. Its "grog shops," writes Elmer Jackson "were dives of vice and rendezvous of the ruffians, murderers and bullies of a rare type."[16] During Upshur's tenure, a midshipman was stabbed in the chest by one of these "street rowdies." Youth gangs from Eastport and Annapolis were known to brawl, often over each others' girls. If Annapolis had a large dose of southern gentility, it also had some of its violence.

The midshipmen were likely more interested in the girls who visited the Yard than those fought over by the town gangs. An 1860 entry in the Duty Officer's Log reads:

> Many ladies honored the yard with their presence in the afternoon much to the delight of the midshipmen who true to their uniforms have a great fondness for the fair sex.[17]

The ladies of Annapolis graced the numerous soirees held in the Academy mess hall, and each year a Winter Ball, held under "banners and trophies captured in blood," marked the holiday season.[18] Learning social niceties such as dancing was more than just recreation for the midshipmen, it was part of their education. "Show me the man who can't dance," said Rear Admiral Edward Simpson (formerly of the Spirits Club), "and you point to a man who is not up in all branches of his profession."[19] The professional education in dancing must have been pleasant, given the renown of Annap-

---

[16]Jackson, *Annapolis*, p. 135.
[17]*Journal of the Officer of the Day*, 7 February 1860.
[18]Marshall, *History of the United States Naval Academy*, p. 86. According to Alfred Thayer Mahan, army officers were not liked by Annapolitans. "Army officers labor under a disadvantage in this place." Robert Seager and Doris D. Maguire, eds., *Letters and Papers of Alfred Thayer Mahan*, vol. 1: *1847–1889* (Annapolis: U.S. Naval Institute Press, 1975), p. 62.
[19]Karsten, *The Naval Aristocracy*, p. 31.

olis "for the beauty and grace of its women."[20] A lively social life also existed within the Naval Academy community. The midshipmen were allowed to visit the homes of the officers and professors any time of the day, except during study hour. Many used this liberty to skip the evening meal in the mess hall. The wife of Superintendent George Blake was especially kind in providing the motherly touch. According to George Dewey, "Mrs. Blake had a warm place in the hearts of all the Annapolis graduates of my time. She was very kind to us in a day when the acting midshipmen saw little of home life."[21]

Midshipman Alfred Thayer Mahan was a frequent guest at Commander Craven's table, where he came to be quite enamored of Nannie Craven, the commandant's daughter. The good commander would often misread his clock so that young Mahan might stay for a while longer, prompting the appreciative midshipman to quip, "Damme, if I know which I like best, father or daughter. . . ."[22] During one evening at the Cravens, a group of midshipmen serenaded the ladies assembled there, who pelted them with apples, "large and hard, [like] regular young round shot."[23] The midshipmen escaped with only wounded pride, surely not the last of their breed to feel the sting of feminine rebuff.

If Annapolis and the Naval Academy enjoyed a warm social relationship they also shared the mutual benefits of the good harbor that made Annapolis Roads the "official gateway to Washington."[24] Diplomats, politicians, foreign vessels, and a variety of noted personages passed through Annapolis, helping the city regain a measure of its former prestige. Officers and midshipmen of the Royal Dutch Navy visited the Academy in 1852 aboard the frigate *Prince of Orange* and were hosted by their American counterparts. In March 1859, the HMS *Curacoa* arrived in Annapolis with the new British minister to the United States, Lord Lyons, on board. He was received with an eleven-gun salute and "all due honor and civility."[25] Lord Lyons was en route to Washington to relieve Lord Napier, who the year before had visited the Naval Academy. In January 1852, a foreigner of a different ilk, the Hungarian revolutionary Louis Kossuth, visited Annapolis and spoke at the Governor's Mansion. The midshipmen were permitted to attend. In April 1856, the new American steam frigate *Merrimac* dropped anchor in Annapolis harbor. It was visited by officers, midshipmen, townspeople, the naval

---

[20]Riley, *The Ancient City*, p. 274.

[21]Dewey, *Autobiography*, p. 20. Mrs. Blake was the daughter of Commodore James Barron who killed Stephen Decatur in a duel.

[22]West, *Admirals of American Empire*, p. 21.

[23]Seager and Maguire, *Letters and Papers of Alfred Thayer Mahan*, p. 16.

[24]Puleston, *Annapolis*, p. 88.

[25]Seager and Maguire, *Letters and Papers*, p. 70.

but a short jump to the idea that the officer's "mission" was "to tame the wild earth" through the spreading of American trade, republicanism, and Christianity.[32] As evidence, Karsten cites Mahan's view that the United States could acquire colonies if it was "the expression of God's Being and God's Will."[33] Thus, naval force could be used in good conscience:

> "I thought I was carrying out the expressed wishes of the Christian people of America," Captain L. M. Overstreet remarked of his part in the Spanish-American and First World Wars, adding that this feeling had been formed "each Sunday morning" in the church of his youth.[34]

The leap from Episcopalianism at the Naval Academy to the Spanish American War is a bold one. Undoubtedly, the Academy's religious training had some effect on the philosophical leanings of its graduates. But there is danger in making too much of it. Alfred Thayer Mahan, cited by Karsten, is a good example. Deeply religious in later life, Mahan was irreverent as a midshipman and strongly critical of Chaplain Jones, also known as "Slicky." He described one of Jones's sermons as "most delightfully and successfully stupid . . . it gave me a most unlovely idea of religion generally." Following a sermon on "Drunkenness," Mahan wrote, "I believe I would give a year's pay to see Old Slicky tight and limber as a rag." As for the "Rum Drinking" sermon, "It is really the most disagreeable thing in the world to sit quietly and listen to the rant and cant of that intolerable old poker." And in response to the sermon entitled "Almost Thou Persuadest me to be a Christian," Mahan mocked,

> it is impossible to convey to you an idea of the comedy. Old Blake began to shift rather uneasily in his seat toward the end, and I should wonder if Slicky got a rap over the knuckles. . . . [The school needs a] decent parson. . . . There is certainly a large field perfectly innocent of cultivation.[35]

Mahan resisted the efforts of ethics Professor Joseph E. Nourse ("Holy Joe") to recruit him for the Bible class, which he ridiculed in letters to Ashe: "Looking at the members of the Bible Class . . . what one of them can we respect?"[36] Neither did Mahan nor the other midshipmen respect a visiting Presbyterian minister's hell, fire, and damnation sermon:

> I can't stand what looks like an effort to bully you into religion. . . . A

---

[32]Ibid., p. 226.
[33]Ibid.
[34]Ibid., p. 223.
[35]Seager and Maguire, *Letters and Papers*, p. 30.
[36]Ibid., p. 31.

man who is religious because he fears to go to hell is as despicable as one who remains irreligious because he fears the world's opinions.[37]

Others besides Mahan were lacking in piety. Midshipman Mish made a drunken spectacle of himself one morning in Chapel during Upshur's tenure, one of a number of midshipmen who praised the Lord while passing the bottle. Upshur described the midshipmen's conduct in church as "ungenteel, unofficerlike, irreverant and I presume . . . also unlawful in the state of Maryland."[38] One of the Academy's regulations punished indecent behavior at church with dismissal from the service, an indication that decency would come only through deterrence. There were, of course, many midshipmen whose behavior was directed by the Holy Spirit, rather than the liquid variety. Mahan described two of his classmates' reactions to Jones's sermons: "Poor Jim O'Kane gets a tearing every Sunday and as for Dunker Ames words cannot do justice to the expression on his face."[39]

Not all of the midshipmen attended the Academy Chapel. At the request of the parents of midshipmen who wanted to attend a church of their choice in town, the Navy Department granted this privilege. Midshipman Mahan remained loyal to Chaplan Jones: "I had rather go to Slicky than walk into town for nothing."[40] What is important is that church attendance *somewhere* was required. Whether that fact supports the Karsten view that Academy indoctrination "carefully preserved religious memories" or that compulsion was a prerequisite for piety, is not easily answered. There would seem to be some evidence that the Academy's religious training was more diverse and less overpowering than Peter Karsten intimates. To whatever extent the Naval Academy Chapel would become the "heart of the Naval Service"[41] in later years, it was but a small part of the service in its infancy.

MORAL EDUCATION

Any system of education to merit approval must promote physical development, patriotism, good morals, and love of law and order.

So spoke Captain Ira L. Reeves, U.S. Army, in *Military Education in the United States* in 1914.[42] Perhaps he was echoing Franklin Buchanan's call for men of obedience, moral character, and temperance at the opening of the

---

[37]West, *Admirals of American Empire*, p. 19.
[38]Upshur to Cornelius McSean, 22 March 1849, "Records of the Naval Academy."
[39]Seager and Maguire, *Letters and Papers*, pp. 33–34.
[40]Ibid., p. 57.
[41]Karsten, *The Naval Aristocracy*, p. 74.
[42]Ira L. Reeves, *Military Education in the United States* (Burlington, Vermont: Free Press Printing Co., 1914), p. 36.

Alfred Thayer Mahan, however, claimed that hazing was nonexistent before the Civil War:

> Not only was hazing not practised [*sic*], but it scarcely obtained even the recognition of mention; it was not so much reprobated as ignored; and if it came under discussion at all, it was dismissed with a turn of the nose as something altogether beneath us. That is not the sort of thing we do here. It may be all very well for West Point; much as "what would do for a marine could not be thought of for a seaman"; but we were officers and gentlemen.[65]

Academy historians Park Benjamin and William Puleston side with Mahan; Peter Karsten, of course, agrees with Dewey. Mahan's recollections were based on letters as a midshipman. Dewey was writing only from memory. On the other hand, Mahan entered the Academy as a third classman—having skipped plebe year. As examples of hazing, Karsten offers Mahan's being placed in "Coventry" and Midshipman Henry D. Foote's being tarred and feathered—both by their classmates. Mahan's Coventry was a kind of "social ostracism" that he suffered after reporting a classmate for talking in ranks. Foote's fate stemmed from his having severely beaten a Negro woman servant within the Yard. Since they involved members of the same class, however, these incidents are not good examples of hazing, which is usually thought of as indoctrination by upperclassmen. Similarly, the enforcement of the Academy's regulations by its officers would not be considered hazing either, especially if it is true that officer-student relations were characterized by "a general good humored tolerance."[66] This tolerance was probably more marked with the oldsters because of their quasi-officer status. William Puleston claims they were "mature midshipmen" who "scorned such sophomoric activities."[67] Perhaps it was not maturity, but rather an exaggerated sense of personal honor that made hazing repugnant to the oldsters. All sources agree that hazing was rampant during the Academy's stay at Newport, Rhode Island, during the Civil War. But if hazing existed in the years before, my guess is that it was minimal.

A stronger force than hazing may have been the feelings of camaraderie, association, and class and service loyalty that Academy life engendered. As Mahan noted:

> I believe that those [friendships and associations] formed at this place or West Point must be far more lasting and deep than those made elsewhere,

[65]Mahan, "Old Times At the Naval Academy," p. 373.

[66]Ibid., p. 374.

[67]William D. Puleston, *Mahan: The Life and Work of Captain Alfred Thayer Mahan, U.S.N.* (New Haven: Yale University Press, 1939), p. 20.

for here we are from every cause brothers, our association, our hopes, our profession all the same.[68]

Peter Karsten maintains that the Academy experience molded the midshipmen into a "band of brothers," intensely loyal to each other, the Academy, and the service. The military profession has always possessed great corporateness, what with its limited membership, traditions, and separation from civilian life.[69] Academy life encourages this. According to Lebby's study, ceremonies, formations, changes of commands, and so forth, "serve to reinforce the sense of group identity fostered by the Academy . . . [and] to heighten the feeling among midshipmen that they are members of a select fraternity sharing a common bond."[70] Thomas O. Selfridge, the Academy's first real "graduate," spoke of this feeling during his era:

> None but a naval officer could fully understand the devotion of another officer to their common service. The close unity of thought and action that binds our profession into a great fraternity has no parallel among civilians.[71]

But even these feelings had limits. While Edward Simpson would compare the Academy to home in terms of the care, guidance, development, character, and principle it gave its graduates, Caspar Goodrich claimed that "the average [Annapolite] respects his Alma Mater but he does not love her as Yalensians love Old Yale."[72] There is a reason why midshipmen count the days until graduation and literally leap with joy after the traditional toss of their caps. Academy life can be quite an ordeal. The 1850s were no different, given poor accommodations, lack of recreational facilities, sparse liberty, and long separations from home. While the unpleasantness of Academy life in its formative years may have helped to draw the midshipmen together, it had some centripetal effects. Only a week before he had spoken of the "lasting" and "deep" associations and friendships engendered at the Academy, Mahan labeled one of his classmates "contemptible," another as an "intriguer and weak," and another as a "damned grinning ass." He referred to the group as his "enemies." For their part, Mahan's classmates "sized him up as a pillar of conceit."[73] The numerous duels and fights described in earlier chapters might also be considered evidence against the "band of brothers" proposition. It would be wrong to make too much of the personal rivalries of adolescent midship-

[68]Seager and Maguire, *Letters and Papers*, p. 9.

[69]Huntington, *Soldier and State*, p. 16.

[70]Lebby, "Professional Socialization," pp. 73–74.

[71]Thomas O. Selfridge, *Thomas O. Selfridge, Jr., Rear Admiral U.S.N.* (New York: G. P. Putnam's Sons, 1924), pp. 286–87.

[72]Lovette, *School of the Sea*, p. 203.

[73]West, *Admirals of American Empire*, p. 19.

men. But it is also a mistake to attribute too much influence to a still-infant Academy. Moreover, if Janowitz is correct in his claim that it is the "physical and historical surroundings that produce the most lasting impressions,"[74] then the interaction of midshipmen may not have been as important a factor in the molding of attitudes as Karsten would have us believe. In fact, the Civil War may have been a far more potent force in shaping the attitudes and ideals of latter-nineteenth-century naval officers than their Naval Academy training. Karsten himself speaks of how that conflict turned "individualistic, anti-institutionalists into men who took great pride in a life of service,"[75] a point that lends credence to Janowitz's view of professional socialization as a gradual process that can be "deeply affected by particular significant and highly charged events."[76] This may be why Lebby's study found that modern midshipmen have a "sense of shared identity" but not a monolithic attitude and value structure.[77] They may simply have not experienced the equivalent of the Civil War.

Annapolis Ideals

> My findings reveal racism, authoritarianism, warmongering, navalism, and a number of other unattractive qualities in the officer corps . . . .
> Its primary loyalty was to the Service—"the Navy, first, last and always." Its secondary loyalty was to the Nation—"my country, right or wrong."
>
> Peter Karsten

The idea that the Civil War, which had at least something to do with notions of nationalism and equality, produced a racist, warmongering, and navalist officer corps begs elaboration. Our inquiry, however, is whether the Academy embodied these characteristics.

To some extent it undoubtedly did. Of racism, for example, a Midshipman McGary called James Holliday a "damned black son of a bitch" and threatened to break his neck and to give him a "damned thrashing" over a minor mail delivery problem. Recounting the incident to Commodore Shubrick, George Upshur described Holliday as a free black of "great respectability, sobriety, and rectitude of conduct, and is remarkable for his close attention to duty as for his uniformly, respectful, humble, and submissive deportment to his superiors."[78] Whether McGary's verbal

---

[74]Janowitz, *The Professional Soldier*, p. 131.
[75]Karsten, *The Naval Aristocracy*, p. 45.
[76]Janowitz, *The New Military*, p. 115.
[77]Lebby, "Professional Socialization," p. 192.
[78]Upshur to Shubrick, 21 August 1847, "Records of the Naval Academy."

assault or Upshur's "Uncle Tom" defense of Holliday was the more racist is difficult to judge. Either would be matched by Thomas G. Ford's characterization of the midshipmen's pet monkey, "Rory," as an African cousin of the Academy's Negro servants, or by Naval Surgeon Solomon Sharpe's beating with a cane of Lieutenant William H. Parker's "negro girl." The Old Naval Academy certainly had its racist elements, especially when judged by today's standards. In the 1850s, however, it was a reflection of the nation as a whole.[79]

Authoritarianism, too, was present at the Academy. Defending Napoleon, Midshipman Mahan claimed that "every great man that ever lived had the nature of a despot." A republic, wrote Mahan,

> . . . is the damndest thing ever created for times when war is even a bare possibility . . . our God damned American independence forbids us to cultivate the great virtue that alone will save us in the hour of danger, obedience—passive, unresisting obedience.[80]

Obedience of the passive, unresisting variety was certainly a goal of every ship's captain in the Old Navy. A moment's delay by a sailor reefing sail in a storm might lose the ship, providing some justification for the "captain is king" tradition. At the Academy, Benjamin Totten's *Naval Textbook . . . for the Use of Midshipmen of the U.S. Navy* spoke of the need for "unbending discipline" and "unhesitating subordination."[81] Demerits and restriction awaited the errant. Obedience, or "fealty" to one's commander, was part of an officer's code of honor. To be obeyed was a prerogative of rank, and in the Old Navy rank counted for much. Even the chaplains were known to report midshipmen for violating regulations.

It would be convenient if the story of the Old Navy Academy was one of obedient midshipmen. In point of fact, however, the disobedience and independence of the midshipmen has been one of the major themes of this study. Fighting, duelling, drinking, smoking, insubordination, vandalism, and worse were commonplace. It is difficult to find any "fealty" in Henry Lockwood's being hanged in effigy, in Midshipman Henry

---

[79]Citing the example of Josiah Tatnall, a Georgian, having Liberian officials dine on his vessel, Daniel Ammen claims that naval officers' wide travel made them less racist than others. Ammen once believed that Negroes "were made to be slaves," but later concluded that slaveowners suffered more than slaves. Daniel Ammen, *The Old Navy and the New* (Philadelphia: J. B. Lippincott Co., 1891), p. 224. Writing in 1870 from West Point to his North Carolina friend, Sam Ashe, Mahan spoke of a "nigger cadet here at the Point." Two years earlier he had written to Ashe: "I am not myself desirous of bolting the entire negro—and hope somewhat sanguinely, that the ultraism of the Radicals may work out deliverance." Seager and Maguire, *Letters and Papers*, pp. 355, 338.

[80]Ibid., p. 72.

[81]Karsten, *The Naval Aristocracy*, p. 35.

given new life in 1828 with the issuance of the Yale Report, a response to the demands of reformers. Its convincing defense of the tools and aims of classical education ensured that "the American college would continue to serve its essentially aristocratic purpose."[98]

And so it did for decades. Catering largely to the sons of well-to-do Bostonians, Harvard did not open its doors to the sons of wage earners until near the turn of the century.[99] When Charles Eliot became its president in 1869, Harvard drew some 95 of its 115 incoming freshmen from private schools. Although known as a reformer, Eliot spoke in 1874 of Harvard's need for the children of "professors, ministers, country physicians, [and] lawyers." In 1886, one of every eight Harvard students was the son of a graduate.[100]

But Harvard was not alone. Princeton boasted the sons of wealthy southern planters, and the class that entered the new University of the City of New York in 1832 read like a "Who's Who" of New York society. As late as 1908, 68 percent of Yale's students had come from private schools.[101]

Elitism was not confined to the Ivy League. In 1825 the governor of Kentucky denounced state support of Transylvania College, saying that "the only result is to add to the aristocracy of wealth, the advantage of superior knowledge."[102] Indiana College was accused of aristocratic tendencies by the local press in 1829, and in 1850 the president of the University of Michigan complained of "cheapened education . . . within the reach of everyone."[103] From South Carolina to Missouri, people equated university students with family wealth. Indeed, elitism permeated even the top of university structure. As Frederick Rudolph writes,

> . . . the sound, conservative men of wealth who came to dominate the college governing boards were pillars of the better classes, and while their duties permitted them to perform a social responsibility, their authority

[98]Ibid., p. 134. Of the collegiate way, President Porter of Yale said, "Let any reflecting man think for a moment of . . . the trickery of business, the jobbery of politicians, the slang of newspapers, the vulgarity of fashion, the sensationalism of popular books, the shallowness and cant that dishonor pulpit and defile worship, and he may reasonably rejoice that there is one community which for a considerable period takes into its keeping many of the most susceptible and most promising of our youth, to impart to them better tastes, higher aims, and, and, above all, to teach them to despise all sorts of intellectual and moral shams."

[99]Hugh Hawkins, *Between Harvard and America: The Educational Leadership of Charles Eliot* (New York: Oxford University Press, 1972), p. 10.

[100]Ibid., pp. 172, 174. This compares roughly with the percentage of midshipmen who were the sons of officers.

[101]Seymour Martin Lipset and David Riesman, *Education and Politics at Harvard* (New York: McGraw Hill, 1975), p. 74.

[102]Rudolph, *The American College and University*, p. 206.

[103]Ibid., p. 63.

also enabled them to keep the colleges true to the interests and prejudices of the classes from which they were drawn.[104]

If elitist tendencies at the Naval Academy reflected those of American colleges in general, they were also mirrored at West Point. As at Annapolis, politics was the culprit. The Point's first superintendent, Captain Alden Partridge, complained of political influence in the appointments process in 1815. Sons of congressmen, senators, cabinet officers, governors, Supreme Court justices, and a vice president studded the long gray line. Robert E. Lee was the son of Harry "Light Horse" Lee of Revolutionary War fame; Rufus King (Class of 1833) the son of the president of Columbia University; Schuyler Hamilton (Class of 1841) the grandson of Alexander Hamilton; and George B. Crittenden (Class of 1832) the son of Senator John Crittenden of Kentucky.[105] And the list goes on. A strong eastern orientation existed among the cadets, as most of the entrance examination failures were from the south and the west. Those surviving the entrance examination, graduating high in their class, and returning as instructors were most likely to be easterners. In 1840, all of the professors and twelve of seventeen assistant professors were from the east. An Act of Congress in 1843 required that cadets be distributed equally among congressional districts, but they still "tended to come from families of importance."[106] Criticized as a "retreat for the pampered sons of the rich," and as being "wholly inconsistent with the spirit and genius of our liberal institutions,"[107] West Point was in many ways aristocratic.

Thus the elitist label on Annapolis, though justified, deserves considerable qualification when viewed in the light of a politicized appointments process and the upper-class makeup of other American colleges. The crops of students harvested by the various mills of higher education were grown in the same fields. As for the criticism, implicit in the Karsten thesis, of the Annapolis ideals of obedience, courage, honor, service, loyalty, and patriotism, no apology is needed. These traits, in proper proportion, are no more inherently bad than antinavalism and pacifism are inherently good. Those who write of the overpowering influence of service academy life often reflect a viewpoint that itself was formed of some overpowering educational influence—for instance, the University of Wisconsin in the 1960s.

---

[104]Ibid., p. 173.

[105]Bruce K. Galloway and Robert Bowie Johnson, *West Point: America's Power Fraternity* (New York: Simon and Schuster, 1973), p. 142.

[106]Ambrose, *Duty, Honor, Country*, p. 130.

[107]Thomas J. Fleming, *The Men and Times of the United States Military Academy* (New York: William Morrow and Co., Inc., 1969), p. 51; Sidney Forman, *A History of the United States Military Academy* (New York: Columbia University Press, 1950), pp. 64–65.

I submit, however, that Academy life in the 1850s—and now—is not the overwhelming force that Karsten and others claim it to be. If midshipmen are impressionable during their academy years they are also rebellious. As an Annapolite myself, I have often observed that the finished product, the graduate, is more a function of the raw material than the manufacturing process. Or as former Academy Superintendent Rear Admiral James Calvert put it, "The Navy is a reflection of the society it exists to defend." In the nineteenth century, American colleges used the collegiate way and a classical curriculum to produce graduates of strong character, good morals, and refinement. The antebellum Naval Academy relied on the Annapolis environment, genteel society, navy tradition, discipline, and moral education to produce officers and gentlemen. If there was a "mainstream" of American life and higher education in the nineteenth century, the Naval Academy was more in than out of it.

CHAPTER SEVEN
SUMMER CRUISES

About noon of the 11th the merry notes of the boatswain's whistle, and the stirring cry of "all hands up anchor," went like an electric thrill throughout the ship; and then there was a hurrying to and fro, as every man sought his station. In a trice the ropes were led along the decks, the capstan bars manned, and to the stirring notes of the fife, we soon "walked the anchor up." Slowly her head swung round; then "sheeting home," her large sails filled, and she bore away from the Academy in handsome style.

A midshipman's account of the departure of the 1860 summer cruise.

If the romance of the age of sail was one reason why young boys chose Annapolis, summer cruise offered them the first real taste of life at sea. Left behind were memories of the classroom, the placid Chesapeake, and genteel Annapolis. The quarterdeck, the unruly Atlantic, and foreign ports beckoned. No longer would the midshipmen's view of naval life and the world be limited to that gained from the literature of the sea and world travellers who passed by the school. With a breeze at their back and salt spray in their face, the midshipmen themselves were now the world travellers. For an Ohio lad whose world view had heretofore extended only to the bend in the river, and to whom a passing flatboat had once been cause for excitement, summer cruise must have been quite an experience.

But summer cruises were important in other ways. Rear Admiral David Dixon Porter claimed that "in every capacity in which a naval officer is placed, seamanship must take precedence of everything else."[1] Midshipmen who entered the Academy prior to the advent of the four-year course in 1851 got their seamanship training during their three-year stint at sea prior to the lieutenant's exam. Those who came after had only summer cruise.

To silence critics and to ensure the success of the four-year program, the Academy had to demonstrate that its summer cruise could train the midshipmen to sail and fight a ship. At stake was the whole concept of formal naval education ashore.

---

[1]Ford Manuscript, Ch. 26, p. 4.

The practice ship *Preble*, vessel for midshipmen at-sea training on seven of the 1850s cruises. Her midshipmen were the latter day *"Preble's Boys."* Courtesy: U.S. Naval Academy Special Collections, Nimitz Library

The idea of a practice cruise was not new in 1851. Commodores Bainbridge and Rodgers, Lieutenants Maury and Powell, Chaplain Jones, and Professor Chauvenet had all advocated it, perhaps because of the success of West Point's well-known summer encampment.[2] But when the Academy was established in 1845, it did not even have a practice ship assigned. The pleas of Superintendents Buchanan and Upshur for a practice ship, and of others for a practice cruise, were finally answered with the 1850 reorganization, which instituted the four-year course with summer cruise and called for the stationing of a practice ship at the Academy. In place were all the elements of the modern Naval Academy, and over the years the value of the summer cruises has proved immense. They are, according to Thomas G. Ford, "the very soul of the system, without which the Academy at Annapolis would inevitably decline."[3]

The First Summer Cruise

The commandant of midshipmen, Lieutenant Thomas Tingey Craven, commanded the first summer cruise in 1851 as well as the cruises of 1852–54 and, as a commander, the cruises of 1858–60. The responsibilities of any sea command are heavy. Craven had the additional burden of making midshipmen into capable mariners and, as a result, proving the efficacy of the summer-cruise concept. A "cool, bold, and skillful seaman and navigator" and "one of the finest sailor-men in the Navy,"[4] Craven succeeded in his task and eventually became a rear admiral. If there is one man who deserves credit for putting the Academy's summer-training program on a steady course, it was Thomas Tingey Craven. His contribution to the Academy and the service was considerable.

Perhaps Craven's greatest challenge was in getting the 1851 cruise underway. For a while the issue was in doubt. Organizational problems delayed the cruise for nearly two months. It was not until 21 July that the ninety midshipmen, along with Craven, Lieutenant R. L. Tilghman (the executive officer), Passed Midshipman J. I. Waddell, Master Samuel Marcy, Purser J. A. Semple, Surgeon M. Duvall, and Professor Henry Lockwood boarded the steamer *John Hancock* at Annapolis and were transported to New York City. These few days on the *John Hancock* represented the sum total of midshipmen-at-sea training in steam propulsion before the Civil War.

On 25 July, all hands, plus a few seamen and a guard of marines, boarded the *Preble*, "ready in every respect to sail." But Craven and the *Preble* were

[2]Puleston, *Annapolis*, p. 70.
[3]Ford Manuscript, Ch. 26, p. 51.
[4]Ibid.; Puleston, *Annapolis*, p. 70.

Thomas Tingey Craven, the man most responsible for the success of the summer cruise program. He ran the practice ship aground on the 1851 cruise, but enjoyed smoother sailing on the six other cruises he commanded prior to the Civil War. Courtesy: U.S. Naval Academy Archives

detained by Captain W. D. Salter, commanding officer of the Brooklyn Navy Yard, because of some "Cuban excitement." Craven wrote to Stribling on 1 August that he feared the cruise would not get out of New York Harbor.[5] On 5 August, however, Salter forwarded to Craven a 2 August communication from the secretary of the navy ordering the *Preble* "to proceed to sea at as early a day as practicable."[6] Within a few hours, *Preble* was gotten underway and towed to the quarantine grounds off Staten Island where it anchored for the night to await daylight and a favorable wind and tide. At daylight on 6 August, the *Preble* and her eager crew made sail and were soon outside of Sandy Hook. The Naval Academy's first summer cruise was underway at last.

Barely two days later the *Preble* ran aground. Using celestial observation, the *Preble's* master, Samuel Marcy, had computed the ship's longitude on 7 August and placed her position some fifteen to twenty miles east of the midshipmen's dead reckoning position. Marcy attributed the difference to the current and to faulty midshipmen navigation. That night the *Preble* struck bottom at eighteen feet, and when daylight broke and the fog lifted Marcy and crew found themselves on the southern shoals of Nantucket Island barely five miles distant. A humiliated Marcy accepted the blame. "Nothing was then left me but the mortifying conclusion that I had made a mistake in my observations or some of my computations," he reported to Craven, and said that it was only through "providential interference that my entirely inexcusable carelessness did not result in a more serious mishap."[7] As the commanding officer, Lieutenant Craven felt himself responsible too:

> This untoward event of being so far out of my reckoning, has, I assure you Sir, been a source of deep mortification to me, and my chagrin was heightened when Mr. Marcy informed me . . . that he had discovered an error in his book—he, poor fellow has suffered much—and though he attributes all the blame to himself, I cannot but feel that some portion of it should fall upon me.[8]

Craven signaled for a pilot and the *Preble* was soon out of danger, having politely refused the assistance of a steamer dispatched to the scene by the Nantucket Steamboat Company. The *Boston Post* listed the *Preble's* grounding under "Marine Disasters." It was nearly a disaster for the Naval Academy.

[5]Craven to Stribling, 1 August 1851, "Records of the Naval Academy."

[6]Craven to Stribling, 1 October 1851, Report on 1851 Cruise, "Records of the Naval Academy."

[7]Marcy to Craven, 16 August 1851, "Records of the Naval Academy."

[8]Craven to Stribling, 18 August 1851, "Records of the Naval Academy."

The rest of the cruise was smoother sailing. The *Preble* stopped at Eastport and Portland in Maine; Portsmouth, New Hampshire; Boston; New London, Connecticut; and Norfolk, Virginia, affording the midshipmen the opportunity to visit dockyards, drydocks, ships, machine shops, rigging lofts, and other marine facilities. Between ports the midshipmen were instructed in seamanship, navigation, and gunnery. Writing from Maine, Craven spoke of officers and crew being pleased with the cruise, and he praised the crew as "the most orderly I have ever met with."[9] Even had the "old law" (flogging) been in effect, wrote Craven, "there has no offense occurred which would have justified punishment by whipping."[10] The *Preble* returned to Annapolis on 27 September, barely two months after it had left.

On 1 October Craven made his formal report to Stribling. Although it spoke of a few problems, most notably bad weather and the want of navigational instruments and textbooks, it gave on the whole a glowing report of the midshipmen's performance and a strong endorsement of the summer cruise concept. Craven described the midshipmen's progress as "exceedingly satisfactory"—"some of the young gentlemen show extraordinary aptitude in the acquirement of every branch of practical knowledge, and all have made far greater progress in the essentials of their profession than usually results from an ordinary cruise of a year." Especially noteworthy was the midshipmen's performance in gunnery. "The precision and accuracy with which the guns were directed," said Craven, "was a subject of general remark—the oldest seamen expressing great surprise that boys so young should so far excel themselves in the practice of this highly important branch of the Naval profession."[11] As for the summer cruise concept, Craven labeled it "eminently successful":

> It has shown, satisfactorily to my mind, that the four year course of instruction at the Academy . . . will afford the student opportunities for acquiring far more in the essential parts of the Naval profession than can be expected from the old system, by six years constant serving in the capacity of a midshipman, without the detailed elementary instruction taught on board of the Practice Ship.[12]

Craven's strong words were echoed in Stribling's own report to the secretary of the navy. "The practicality of giving thorough instruction on board the practice ship . . . has been fully proved . . . no actual service as a Midshipman on board a man of war could possibly be so efficacious."[13]

[9]Craven to Stribling, 18 August 1851, "Records of the Naval Academy."
[10]Craven to Stribling, 1 September 1851, "Records of the Naval Academy."
[11]Craven to Stribling, 1 October 1851, "Records of the Naval Academy."
[12]Ibid.
[13]Tisdale, "A Cruise," p. 368.

Cruise Life: At Sea

With the success, and lessons, of the 1851 cruise as a guide, Lieutenant Craven developed an organization and training routine for summer cruises that changed little until 1909, the year of the last summer cruise on a sailing ship.[14] Upon the completion of exams in June, the first and third class midshipmen were boarded onto the practice ship; assigned watch stations, lockers, and mess seats; and divided into gun crews. Four gun crews manned the guns, the fifth (also called the powder division) supplied ammunition, and the sixth (the master's division) acted as quartermasters, helmsmen, and lookouts. The midshipmen were further divided into port and starboard watches. While on watch, the midshipmen answered orders such as trimming, furling, or reefing sails, fueling the galley, bracing the yards, and tacking or wearing the ship. The deck watch, in addition, drilled for three hours in marlinspike seamanship, while the below watch studied navigation. At 4:00 P.M. all hands mustered at station for man-overboard, fire, collision, and abandon-ship drills. The first class midshipmen took turns as officer of the deck and navigator. In all, a midshipman was on deck watch every day for six hours, not counting drills, and for four hours every three nights of four. Every fourth night he spent an "all night" in his hammock which had only twelve inches swinging room. With such a strenuous regimen, they doubtless slept well.[15]

Even though it was a practice cruise, the dangers inherent in sea life were still very real, a fact which made for good training.[16] More often than not, the midshipmen ran the practice ship aground in Annapolis harbor shortly after getting underway. "An interesting event to the nautical critics who watched the maneuver from the river front of the Academy,"[17] it provided a good lesson in seamanship. Once underway, storms and gales were the teachers, as Craven described in his report on the 1860 cruise:

> During a pretty smart gale, which occurred on the 13th inst., one of our topsails was split; this occasion was taken advantage of to practice the acting midshipmen in shifting topsails—and while at anchor in the Patuxent another fresh blow afforded the opportunity for practicing them at sending down royal, topgallant and topsail yards—sending down topgallant masts and striking topmasts—getting off and on caps and cross trees. The young gentlemen have also been taught practically how to carry out a heavy anchor between two boots, and to heave the ship off after she had "taken the ground."[18]

[14]Puleston, *Annapolis*, p. 75.
[15]Ibid., p. 73.
[16]Between 1845 and 1861, the navy lost sixteen ships—none in combat.
[17]Ford Manuscript, Ch. 26, p. 9.
[18]Craven to Blake, 30 September 1860, "Records of the Naval Academy."

But bad weather had its drawbacks, too. On the 1859 cruise, Craven nearly lost the ship. The *Plymouth* had departed from Brest and was just to windward of the most dangerous point on the French coast when a headwind and heavy seas carried away two chain bobstays that were part of the bowsprit rigging. "Had our bowsprit gave on the night in question," Craven wrote to Blake, "we could not possibly have cut clear of the wreck before this ship would have been lost—I thank God for his providence and mercy."[19]

Besides its dangers, stormy weather made training in gunnery and navigation difficult, if not impossible. It also made the midshipmen seasick. Craven spoke of the "general disability" of the midshipmen on the wet and stormy passage from the Chesapeake to Cherbourg in 1858, and according to a midshipman on the 1860 cruise a mere nine knot breeze rendered the lee gangway "as crowded as Washington after a late Presidential election, each sufferer seeming to consider himself more fully entitled to a place than his neighbor."[20] One midshipman who had recovered from the mal de mer approached one of his still-suffering brethren and dangled a huge, molasses-covered piece of fat pork in front of him. "There was a world of indignation in the pale man's looks," a witness described, "and with a wild bound he had well nigh hauled the torturer down the main hatch."[21] The age of sail was not all romance and adventure.

For those boys who were able to eat, a storm at sea posed other problems, as one midshipman recounted:

> During the storm the steerage was the scene of the veriest confusion, as camp stools, crockery and tables, in wild disorder, joined in a general dance to the music of the tempest. At dinner we were seated at table, making desperate efforts to get something to eat, and the servants vainly striving to help us, when a sudden roll sent camp stools and midshipmen pell-mell across the deck, amongst broken dishes, into about a foot of water; the table fastenings giving way at the same time, it and the yet occupied stools went with a crash against the lockers, to the amazement of the seaproof epicureans, who, without suffering interruption, still vainly called for hard tack and tea. It was supremely ridiculous to see them, as totally unmindful of the next lunch, they continued to eat and roar with laughter. On such occasions do we enjoy ourselves most board ship.[22]

The challenge of holding onto one's plate during the ship's dash from the crest of a wave to the trough was likely the only enjoyment the midshipmen

---

[19]Craven to Blake, 1 August 1859, "Records of the Naval Academy."
[20]Ford Manuscript, Ch. 26, pp. 11–12.
[21]Ibid., p. 12.
[22]Ibid., pp. 12–13.

got from eating, for the cruise victuals were bad. "Hard tack, salt junk, pork and beans, weevily rice, wormy cheese, rancid butter,"[23] was Winfield Scott Schley's description of the food on his cruise. No livestock was taken aboard for food, and on the 1851 cruise the midshipmen were not allowed commuted rations. (Commuted rations meant that one received a payment for the value of a meal intead of the meal itself, presumably providing the midshipmen the means to purchase better food while in port.) On the 1852 and later cruises, three of every ten rations were commuted. But even that left the midshipmen half-starved. As Park Benjamin notes, "salt horse and pork, and dirty water from the bottom of tanks, was not an appropriate diet for growing youth."[24] Fresh fish was obtained only occasionally because of orders to keep to sea as long as possible without going into port. On the 1859 cruise, the *Plymouth* obtained some six hundred pounds of codfish and halibut from a French fishing boat on the Banks, but by the time the cruise reached Brest, the midshipmen's stomachs were empty.[25] Since they had little spending money, some of the midshipmen sold their clothing and their sextants in European ports to buy food. It is little wonder that the Academy's purveyor, Colonel Thomas Swann, won the hearts of the midshipmen when, upon the return of one of the cruises, he met the midshipmen at the school gate and took them to his home for dinner.

Rancid food, storms, and seasickness were not the only unpleasant aspects of cruise life. There were also overcrowding, cramped and poorly ventilated quarters, disease, and death. As early as 1852, the Board of Examiners felt the *Preble* was too small. The number of mishipmen on cruise grew throughout the 1850s:

1851–*Preble*	90 Midshipmen and Acting Midshipmen
1852–*Preble*	35 Acting Midshipmen
1853–*Preble*	53 Acting Midshipmen
1854–*Preble*	35 Acting Midshipmen
1855–*Preble*	79 Acting Midshipmen
1856–*Plymouth*	53 Acting Midshipmen
1857–*Preble*	62 Acting Midshipmen
1858–*Preble*	97 Acting Midshipmen
1859–*Plymouth*	107 Acting Midshipmen
1860–*Plymouth*	115 Acting Midshipmen[26]

[23]West, *Admirals of American Empire*, p. 23.
[24]Benjamin, *The United States Naval Academy*, p. 220.
[25]Of the encounter with the French vessel, Craven wrote to Blake: "the poor French man, whom we boarded, was quite happy when our boat left him—as he remarked that he thought war had broken out between England and France and that we were English in disguise." 25 July 1859, "Records of the Naval Academy."
[26]Ford Manuscript, Ch. 26, p. 53.

Each midshipman had a locker barely large enough for a few pieces of clothing and toilet articles and a hammock with only twelve inches swinging room. In such conditions, disease could spread rapidly. There were a few outbreaks of measles, and on one cruise the midshipmen caught the "Portuguese itch" after sending their laundry to some washerwomen on Madeira. They "scratched themselves across the Atlantic."[27] Disease and death were accepted as part of shipboard life. Alfred Thayer Mahan wrote of how personally nonplussed he was when during the 1857 cruise the sergeant of marines died. Upon being told of the death, the first lieutenant's response was, " 'Very well, Sir, report it to the Captain . . . . You must be more careful about those beans'."[28]

Replacing the *Preble* with the larger sloop *Plymouth* on the 1856, 1859, and 1860 cruises eased the overcrowding problem only slightly, since the number of midshipmen was increasing, too. And the *Plymouth* had its own drawbacks. After a thirty-four-day passage to Cadiz on the 1860 cruise, Commander Craven complained to Blake, "the ship sails miserably—and besides having a fine young crop of oysters growing on her bottom the ship is much out of trim."[29] Requests for a sail/steam frigate by superintendents and Boards of Examiners throughout the 1850s went unheeded in Washington, and it was not until 1899 that the USS *Chesapeake* was built solely for training midshipmen.[30] The wooden ship–iron men ethic was slow to die.

Given an oyster-hulled practice ship, bad food, and a host of other inconveniences, summer cruise was no picnic. For some midshipmen, especially those who had entered the navy out of family pressure, one taste of sea life was enough and they "hurried away from what seemed to them a floating prison to the flesh-pots and four-posters of the Academy."[31] But for those with a zest for the naval life, like Alfred Thayer Mahan, cruise was enchanting. "Life at sea, so far as I have experienced it," he wrote,

> is the most happy careless and entrancing life that there is. In a stiff breeze when the ship is heeling well over there is a wild sort of delight that I never experienced before.[32]

[27]Puleston, *Annapolis*, p. 73.
[28]Seager and Maguire, *Letters and Papers*, p. 4.
[29]Craven to Blake, 2 August 1860, "Records of the Naval Academy."
[30]The *Chesapeake* was a steel-hulled square-rigger that served as a cruise ship until 1907. The last cruise in a sailing vessel was in 1909 aboard the *Hartford*, Admiral Farragut's Civil War flagship. Sweetman, *The U.S. Naval Academy* p. 164.
[31]Ford Manuscript, Ch. 26, p. 16.
[32]Seager and Maguire, *Letters and Papers*, p. 4.

Portcalls

Even though most of the time was spent at sea, port visits at home and abroad were an important part of the cruise experience. The 1852 cruise was an island tour, with stops at Fayal in the Azores, Madeira, Santa Cruz and Palma in the Canaries, and St. Thomas in the West Indies. In 1853 the *Preble* cruised in European waters. After touching again at Fayal, the *Preble* dropped anchor in Coruna on the northern coast of Spain where she was "received with the greatest possible kindness and attention" by the governor general of the province and by local authorities. Although his orders did not call for it, Craven took *Preble* and her midshipmen to the great naval arsenal at Ferrol, having "received the most pressing invitation to visit" there. Under the charge of Lieutenant Marcy, the midshipmen made a "highly instructive" tour. "We found everything in great activity within its walls," reported Craven," and were informed that over 3000 artisans and laborers were at work." After departing Ferrol, the cruise stopped in Funchal and, contrary to orders, did not touch at Martinique due to reported sickness there and to the want of time.[33]

The 1854 cruise made "very interesting and instructive" calls at Plymouth, Cherbourg, and Brest. The local dignitaries received them politely and allowed the midshipmen to examine the dockyards, machine shops, and ships. At Brest, the midshipmen toured the French school ship *La Borda*—a kind of floating classroom for sailors. The Americans were impressed:

> Here we were particularly struck with the great care taken to train up expert seamen for their Navy, and the importance attributed to that object . . . . For this purpose there is a large ship, on board of which, such as are destined for the service are taught to read and write, as well as gunnery and seamanship—for this latter branch of instruction, they have two fine Brigs, on board of which from two to three hundred boys, between 13 and 18 years of age are daily exercised in getting underway, manning and taking in sail, reefing and fueling and indeed in all the duties required of thorough seamen. Every six months about one thousand of the best qualified of them are drafted into the naval service.[34]

Commander Joseph F. Green commanded the cruise from 1855–57. The 1855 cruise was a stormy one along the east coast of the United States, with

---

[33]Craven to Stribling, 1 October 1853, "Records of the Naval Academy."

[34]Craven to Goldsborough, 30 September 1854, "Records of the Naval Academy." By comparison, training for American sailors was abysmal. It improved, however, in the 1880s and 1890s—perhaps due in small part to the French example.

stops in Eastport, Portland, Provincetown, and Boston. In Portland, a Mrs. Little gave a ball for the midshipmen which helped to "not only amuse but improve them" by offering a taste of the "polite life" to go with the "rough and tumble experience of a seaman."[35] The 1856 cruise was to Boston, Portland, and Newport aboard the *Plymouth*. *Preble* returned in 1857 for a cruise to Fayal in the Azores.

Thomas T. Craven returned to the Academy as commandant in 1857 and commanded the 1858, 1859, and 1860 cruises. The 1858 cruise met with "boisterous weather" on the passage to Cherbourg, whence *Preble* traveled to Cadiz, where Craven found neither wine for the Academy's superintendent, George Blake, nor mantilla for Blake's wife. He did find the Spanish to be rather inhospitable, as he reported to Blake: "I feel provoked enough at times to wish that we would find some good reason for pitching in to those Spaniards in the Gulf and that I might be one of the helping hands."[36] The next stop was Madeira where Craven was only able to buy wine for himself and his brother, again leaving Blake dry. Upon returning to Hampton Roads, where, in accordance with standard cruise routine, the midshipmen were to have trained for two to three weeks on the smooth waters of the Chesapeake, the *Preble* was ordered to Annapolis so that it could debark the midshipmen and be fitted out for the Paraguay expedition.

The 1859 cruise saw visits to Plymouth, Brest, and Madeira where *Preble* was well received, and a call at Cadiz where *Preble* was quarantined, ostensibly for lack of a bill of health. Craven waited nineteen hours and then "left the port in disgust."[37] Needless to say, he failed for the second year in a row to get George Blake's cherry wine. Perhaps in hope that the third visit would be a charm, Craven planned for a stop in Cadiz on the 1860 cruise. Departing Hampton Roads on 27 June, *Preble* dropped anchor in Horta on the island of Fayal in the Azores on July 17, en route to Cadiz. Though they were on Fayal but a day, the midshipmen made the most of the visit, as one recounted:

> . . . we lost no time; mounting those little donkeys, smaller than Shetland ponies . . . we were soon, many of us, at the summit of the mountain, which contains within it, below the level of the sea, a limpid lake of water, meandering through delicious orange groves.[38]

After a "long and exhausting run of thirteen days," *Preble* reached Cadiz where, just as a year before, she was put in quarantine, this time because of

[35]Franklin, *Memoirs*, p. 146.
[36]Craven to Blake, 15 September 1858, "Records of the Naval Academy."
[37]Craven to Blake, 19 September 1859, "Records of the Naval Academy."
[38]Ford Manuscript, Ch. 20, p. 14.

some supposed sickness at Fayal. The midshipmen were disappointed, but philosophical:

> So it was not permitted us to visit this handsome city, rendered so interesting by history, wherein so many pages inform us of the martial bearing of its sons, the bravery of her defences, and the fierce valor with which the inhabitants of this renowned old city so often met the Moor. Few persons have the opportunity of seeing so beautiful a city with so noble a harbor, on whose bosom rest hundreds of ships.[39]

Finding his third visit in as many years to Cadiz a mortification rather than a charm, Craven made sail for Gibraltar but abandoned that destination for Madeira where, after a "steamboat run" of three days, *Preble* anchored on 2 August. Again it is the midshipman's account that gives a real flavor of this tropical sojourn—and of cruise life:

> Here we remained three brief, swiftly flying days, revelling in the luxuries which generous nature yields in this delightful spot, and exploring the island on horseback. The scenes in the fruitboats that came off to the ship are beyond description, so amusing were they. They would lay around the ship in great numbers until the hour for their coming alongside. The moment the bell would strike they would pounce upon us as if they were meant to board, amidst the yells and cries and imprecations, each boat striving to reach the gangway, and each boatman using his boat hook with vigor upon his neighbor's head . . . . It were impossible to conceive the confusion incident upon a promiscuous buying and selling amongst the "Degos." Our stay proved remarkably pleasant. No one may enjoy the balmy air, listen to gay carols of the beautiful birds flitting lightly from bough to bough, and wander idly through those delightful groves, overlooking fearful chasms, without feeling an inward desire to hold such communes with nature daily and hourly. The more so when weary miles of water separate him from the favorite spot.[40]

After a brief stop at Santa Cruz on the island of Tenerife, *Preble* set sail for home on 10 August and, after a short passage of twenty-three days, dropped anchor in Hampton Roads on 3 September.

Though short in seamanship training, portcalls were of incalculable benefit in broadening the cultural and naval horizons of the midshipmen. Visits to dockyards and arsenals, encounters with Spaniards and "Degos," and pleasant hours passed on island mountains and in lush orange groves, all helped to develop in these young midshipmen a more expansive world view. If the purpose of education is an increased awareness of life's possibilities, summer cruise was a very fine school indeed.

[39]Ibid.
[40]Ibid., p. 15.

Midshipmen Performance

With a few exceptions, the midshipmen's performance on summer cruise was exemplary. Those exceptions, however, merit at least passing comment, for most involved drinking. On the 1853 cruise, Craven offered this report of Midshipmen Quackenbush:

> From all that I can learn he has been behaving himself like almost anything else but a gentleman—there are reports of his having been drunk—and of his enticing some of the youngsters to violate their pledge, and to join him in drinking—I am sorry to say that I cannot obtain the necessary evidence to convict him of his misconduct.[41]

On the 1859 cruise, Midshipmen Ogden, Phoenix, and Bowen were sent to visit a dockyard in *Plymouth*. They returned "three sheets to the wind," with Ogden "so drunk that he was lying in a state of insensibility in the bottom of the boat." Craven accused the three of "behaving themselves like black guards" and recommended Ogden's dismissal.[42] On that same cruise a group of midshipmen went ashore in Brest and returned to the *Plymouth* with long loaves of French bread tucked under their arms. Shortly thereafter these same midshipmen were found intoxicated, and an inspection revealed that they had smuggled bottles of wine aboard ship in the hollowed-out bread loaves.[43] Perhaps this is why Edward Simpson pleaded, "If there is a ship in the service that ought to have a chaplain on board, it is the practice ship."[44]

The story of summer cruise, however, is to be found in the praise heaped upon the midshipmen, rather than in their few transgressions. Describing their skills in gunnery on the 1853 cruise, Craven wrote that

> there was scarcely a shot fired that would not have hulled a frigate at the distance of a mile. Upon one occasion so accurate was the firing that of 15 shot expended the greatest deviation was not more than three feet to the left of the centre of the target. Ten were line shots, and 2 were directly through the centre. The target was at this time from 800 to 1100 yards distant, the ship rolling about two and a half streaks and the swell of the sea nearly if not quite four feet.[45]

---

[41]Craven to Stribling, 19 October 1853, "Records of the Naval Academy."
[42]Craven to Blake, 1 August 1859, "Records of the Naval Academy."
[43]Benjamin, *The United States Naval Academy*, pp. 220–21.
[44]Edward Simpson letter, 17 June 1860, "Records of the Naval Academy." Simpson wrote: ". . . it seems very hard that these young gentlemen, in whom so much interest is felt in all parts of the country, should be turned adrift so young, without some spiritual provision being made for their eternal welfare."
[45]Craven to Stribling, 1 October 1853, "Records of the Naval Academy."

Reporting on the 1854 cruise, Craven rated the midshipmen better gunners than the ship's crew.

On the 1858 cruise, Craven singled out the midshipmen's expeditious response to fire drills for his praise:

> So expert had the young gentlemen become at this drill, that upon a sudden and unexpected alarm of fire, the young gentlemen would be at their stations, as firemen, wreckers and smothering parties, provided with buckets, wet swabs, axes, etc.—the pumps would be rigged, and a full supply of water could be thrown upon any part of the ship in less than five minutes—and all boats would be cleared away and ready for hoisting out in eight minutes.[46]

In 1859 it was excellent midshipmen navigation that impressed Craven. After leaving Madeira for the Chesapeake, the midshipmen first class were divided into parties of six and kept constantly busy at determining ship's position by celestial navigation. To impress upon the midshipmen that the ship's safety was entrusted to them, the ship's master was forbidden to have anything to do with navigation. Craven termed the midshipmen's progress "remarkable" in that after only two days there was seldom more than a one to one-and-a-half minute difference in the work of each midshipman from the mean of their combined observations. So accurate was their navigation that when a lookout was sent aloft after the last course change, Cape Henry light was "exactly aboard." "In all my experience," raved Craven, "I have never made, or known a more perfect landfall . . . there is not a member of the first class who is not at this moment fully capable to navigate a ship."[47]

On the 1860 cruise, Craven praised all of the midshipmen for accomplishing their man-overboard drill in seven minutes and twenty seconds. He was especially impressed with the third class midshipmen who, because of overcrowding at the Academy, had been berthed and taught during the past year aboard the *Plymouth*. Craven attributed their exceptional performance to this new "school ship" system which he labeled as "eminently successful."[48] He may have been echoing the sentiments of his assistant, Lieutenant Edward Simpson, who felt that even if the Academy's enrollment *declined*, "a very long step *backwards* will be made if the fourth class be not kept afloat in a School Ship."[49]

Summer cruises were the single most important aspect of the Naval Academy program in the antebellum era. Besides providing midshipmen with realistic training, a taste of life at sea, and a broadened world view,

[46]Craven to Blake, 20 September 1858, "Records of the Naval Academy."
[47]Craven to Blake, 27 September 1859, "Records of the Naval Academy."
[48]Craven to Blake, 30 September 1860, "Records of the Naval Academy."
[49]Simpson to Craven, 17 June 1860, "Records of the Naval Academy."

they silenced Academy critics and guaranteed the continuance of the four-year program. With their success passed the last chance that the Naval Academy would fail. The concept of formal training ashore had proven its worth and found a permanent home in Annapolis.

Homecomings

While the practice ship usually returned to the Chesapeake in early September for smooth-water training, cruise did not officially end until the midshipmen sighted the old mulberry tree at the Academy upon the return to Annapolis. Midshipmen of the first class had the satisfaction of knowing that their next cruise would be as officers. For the third class, there was the opportunity to tell "salty" tales (in condescending tone) to the newly admitted fourth class midshipmen "whose reverence for the returned mariners was refreshing to behold."[50] For Craven (or Greene) the end of cruise brought relief from the responsibility of sea command. And for the superintendent and the Academy community, the sight of the practice ship in Annapolis Roads meant an end to concern for the safety of ship and men.

These were the thoughts likely evoked by the return of the *Plymouth* to Annapolis in 1860. *Plymouth* would soon be replaced as school ship by that great symbol of union and national honor, the USS *Constitution*—"Old Ironsides." If ever the nation needed such a symbol, it was in the fall of 1860. The slavery question that everyone hoped would go away had been inflamed anew with the pernicious Dred Scott decision, the Lincoln-Douglas debates, and John Brown's raid. As a dangerously divided America faced the upcoming 1860 elections, men of sane counsel hoped for yet another compromise to avoid the issue so clearly posed by the abolitionists. But by 1860, sane voices went unheard. Symbolic of a house divided, four political parties vied for the presidency and the unenviable responsibility of preserving the Ship of State in the moment of its greatest peril. When Abraham Lincoln captured the White House with nary a single southern electoral vote, the United States had its first truly "sectional" president. Their bluff called, southern leaders who had threatened secession if Lincoln was elected made good their pledge. Like a joker in the deck, the long-festering, oft-avoided slavery question was finally face up on the table. The Devil was calling in his chips.

[50]Ford Manuscript, Ch. 26, p. 17.

CHAPTER EIGHT
INTO THE MAELSTROM:
THE END OF
THE OLD NAVAL ACADEMY

We are indeed, in the midst of a Revolution— the results of which no man can foresee. Let us, however, endeavor to hope on, hope ever.

John S. Cunningham
2 May 1860

With the fury of a long-gathering storm, the Civil War unleashed the pent-up energies of forty years of sectional controvery upon the American people, more than six hundred thousand of whom would lose their lives in the conflict. The reasons for the carnage were twofold. The Civil War was the first so-called modern war. It was the first war in which railroads moved large numbers of troops and dictated strategy; in which the new weapons of the industrial revolution—gatling guns, rifled cannon, explosive shells, steam-powered vessels, submarines, and torpedoes—were tested; in which one side's industrial base and mass conscription proved decisive; and in which telegraphic communication and coverage by the press provided daily battle reports to the populace.[1] Though not a "total war" like World War II, the Civil War was a harbinger of the destructive capacity of a modern industrial state.

The second reason lay in the bitterly divisive issues of slavery, nationalism, and states' rights. It was not over a tariff that hundreds of thousands died, but rather over conflicting views of America and Americanism. These irreconcilable differences, combined with each side's view that God, the Constitution, and Destiny were with them, made a fight to the finish inevitable. It was for good reason that Ulysses S. Grant came to command the Union Army. Grant stood for "unconditional surrender."

[1]Some of these factors were also important in the Crimean War a decade earlier, but to a lesser degree.

Nowhere did the strains of the Civil War pull harder than in Maryland, in Annapolis, and at the Naval Academy. A border state whose sympathies were divided between North and South, Maryland was one of the strategic keys of the war, given its proximity to Washington and its location astride the Potomac and the Chesapeake. Would Maryland remain true to the nationalism that was so much a part of its history, or would the state of Fort McHenry and "The Star Spangled Banner" follow the inclinations of its tidewater inhabitants and secede? Had Maryland chosen secession, the Union cause would have been dealt a serious, perhaps fatal, blow.

Annapolis was important for all of these reasons, and others. Besides being the state capital, it possessed a fine harbor (well protected by forts), a steam-railway link to Washington, and a strong southern orientation in its society and culture. This was shown in the 1860 election in which Annapolitans cast 261 votes for Bell, 227 for Breckinridge, 36 for Douglas, and only 1 for Lincoln.[2] Many slaves had entered America at Annapolis, and the city still had a sizable Negro (some of them slaves) population.

Annapolis also had the Naval Academy, a national institution with officers and mishipmen from states north and south. Here were men whose training aimed at making them a band of brothers. The Civil War would test these loyalties. It would also test the resilience of the Academy itself which, forced out of Annapolis by the exigencies of the war, took refuge for four years in Newport, Rhode Island. With its grounds under the control of the army, its graduates shooting at each other, and the nation it represented split, these were perilous times for the Naval Academy. Not since the days of George Upshur was its fate more uncertain.

George S. Blake

Fortunately, the Academy had the steady hand of George Blake at the helm. Blake was born in 1803 in Worcester, Massachusetts, the first Academy superintendent from north of the Mason-Dixon line. A midshipman at the age of fifteen, Blake distinguished himself aboard the schooner *Alligator* which was attacked by a Portuguese vessel near the Cape Verde Islands in 1821. In recognition of his performance, Blake was made executive officer of the captured ship on its voyage back to the United States. Promoted to lieutenant in 1827, he won a commendation from the Navy Department in 1846 for saving the crippled brig *Perry* from destruction in a hurricane off Florida. The next year, Blake made commander, and in 1855 he became a captain. Blake's tour as superintendent from 15 September 1857 to 9

[2]Riley, *The Ancient City*, p. 281.

Captain George S. Blake. Blake's eight-year tenure as superintendent was the longest in Naval Academy history. He and his wife were well-liked by the midshipmen, in whom he took a fatherly interest. He personally answered more than a thousand letters a year from midshipmen's parents. Courtesy: U.S. Naval Academy Archives

September 1865 was the longest in Academy history.[3] Described as "portly" and "dignified," he took pride in claiming to have "never wronged a midshipman."[4] His wife welcomed the midshipmen into their home, and Blake himself took a fatherly interest in them as evidenced by his personally answering more than one thousand letters a year from their parents.[5]

Blake's "First Term"

The first four years of Blake's superintendency roughly coincided with the presidency of James Buchanan. Whereas Buchanan presided over the dissolution of the Union, George Blake oversaw the maturing of the Naval Academy as an institution and its acceptance by the service. By 1861, the Academy "had reached as high a degree of prosperity as the economical policy of Congress permitted."[6]

CONTROLLING THE MIDSHIPMEN

Blake was the first Academy superintendent to have real success in disciplining the midshipmen. It was partly good fortune, for one of the reasons for the school's improved moral tone was the passing of the oldsters. Blake was the first superintendent who did not have to contend with their "pernicious influence."[7] Equally important was the coming to grips with the drinking problem. On 17 May 1858, Secretary of the Navy Isaac B. Toucey issued the following general order:

> Hereafter no commanding officer of any vessel of the United States Navy under whom the graduates of the Naval Academy shall serve will give letters which will entitle them to their final examination, if addicted to the habit of intoxication.[8]

Toucey's order was aimed at midshipmen who had already graduated. The Maryland legislature, however, was looking to those still at the Academy. In 1859, at the behest of Blake and some prominent Annapolitans, the legislature prohibited the sale of liquor to minors. By putting the force of Maryland law behind the school's regulations, this act "removed one of the greatest obstacles to the preservation of order in the Academy."[9] George Upshur could have used this kind of help.

[3]Writers Program of the Works Projects Administration in the State of Maryland, *A Guide to The United States Naval Academy* (New York: The Devin-Adair Company, 1941), p. 56.

[4]Sweetman, *The U.S. Naval Academy*, p. 55.

[5]Ibid.

[6]Ford Manuscript, Ch. 15, p. 25.

[7]Ibid., p. 1.

[8]"Records of the Naval Academy."

[9]Ford Manuscript, Ch. 15, p. 4.

Another reason for Blake's success in reining in the midshipmen was in the system of rewards he devised. Exemplary midshipmen were made the leaders of companies and gun crews, and a star was placed opposite the names of the five outstanding members of each class in the Academy's "Official Register." In 1858 the Navy Department ordered that the register be published annually and distributed among midshipmen's parents and in the service. This led to the star becoming a part of the midshipman uniform and to the tradition of presenting to the man who stood first in his class an inscribed, regulation sword—"a prize highly valued and most eagerly contended for."[10] Lieutenant Christopher R. P. Rodgers, the commandant under Blake, gave this positive approach to discipline a new wrinkle by extending to the first class midshipmen many privileges not granted to the lower classes. In return Rodgers expected the seniors to discipline those below them.

There were, of course, still some problems. Before the new drinking laws took effect, a spate of incidents involving drunken midshipmen had prompted Blake to write of the "terrible rise of intemperance . . . at the Naval Academy."[11] He feared the ruination of many of the finest men in the country and recommended compulsory dismissal for such offenses. As under other previous superintendents, the midshipmen signed numerous drinking pledges to save their classmates threatened with dismissal. "Tobacco pledges" were also exacted from the midshipmen in return for town liberty and for the privilege of escorting young ladies to naval balls. There were even "card pledges."[12] The year 1858 saw a series of vandalism incidents, one involving an explosion set off by the midshipmen in their quarters, and the usual number of midshipmen fights. In 1859 the midshipmen locked up the assistant professor of chemistry, William R. Hopkins (called "Bull Pup"), in a glass cage in his laboratory until he promised to give them all high marks. That year also saw the infamous Foote affair (see page 153).

But all in all, the Naval Academy on the eve of the Civil War had finally gained the ascendancy over its midshipmen. The 1859 Board of Visitors reported that it was "quite struck with the almost entire absence of serious offenses" at the school,[13] bearing out Thomas G. Ford's claim that the Academy had reached a "high point of discipline and efficiency."[14] Given

[10]Ibid., p. 5.
[11]Blake to Toucey, 13 December 1857, "Records of Naval Shore Establishments."
[12]Wrote one apprehended cardster, "And now Capt. Blake I swear to you never to touch another card while I am at the Academy or to play another card while I live." Midshipman Malin to Blake, 11 April 1859, "Records of the Naval Academy."
[13]Report of the Board of Visitors, 17 June 1859, "Records of the Naval Academy."
[14]Ford Manuscript, Ch. 29, p. 51.

the turbulence of the Upshur era barely a decade in the past, this was no small accomplishment.

TAKING POWER FROM THE PROFESSORS

Having made the school more of a military institution in the discipline area, Blake moved in October 1860 to strengthen the power of its officer staff on the Academic Board. Heretofore made up of the superintendent, the commandant, and eight civilian professors, Blake added the commanding officer of the school ship and the assistant instructors of gunnery and seamanship (all sea officers) to the board. To make room, he limited the participation on the board of the professors of French, Spanish, and drawing to matters pertaining only to their subjects. This resulted in a greater emphasis on professional studies, something advocated a year earlier by the midshipmen.[15] Already, the mathematics course had been reduced.[16] The Academy's philosophy of education, long unsettled, was leaning in the direction of making midshipmen sailors, not scholars.

The departure of Professor William Chauvenet from the Academy in August 1859 undoubtedly weakened the civilian professors' influence. In poor health, Chauvenet had initially asked for a year's furlough from the school. The request was granted, but Chauvenet did not return. With offers to teach at several American colleges, Chauvenet accepted a position at Washington University in St. Louis. Within a short time he was made chancellor. His loss was keenly felt in Annapolis. For eighteen years he had been the "central figure in the Academy," a "directing" force with the "power to lift up the institution by degrees as a school of mathematics," a "guide and superior" for the civilian professors. He died in 1870, a renowned American scholar.[17]

THE SCHOOL SHIP

With the influence of sea officers on the rise at the Academy, it seemed only fitting that a ship finally be stationed there. This occurred in 1859 with the *Plymouth*, just returned from summer cruise. The immediate reason for the stationing, however, was overcrowding at the school. Blake had provided for the faculty with the building of five new houses (known as Blake Row)

---

[15]The midshipmen recommended dropping the chemistry course and dividing its time between the departments of seamanship and gunnery.

[16]Thomas G. Ford claims that some of the school's officers in the late 1850s had stood low in their class as midshipmen, "disdained scientific 'truck'," and looked down on the civilian professors—and that this "had a baneful effect upon the midshipmen." Ford Manuscript, Ch. 15, pp. 12–15.

[17]Ford Manuscript, Ch. 15, p. 31. Ford suggests that the Academy's attempts to replace civilian instructors with naval officers was one reason why Chauvenet left the school.

Professor Chauvenet in retirement at his home not long before his death in 1870.
Courtesy: U.S. Naval Academy Archives

and the conversion of the old hospital into a residence. For the 121 new fourth class midshipmen, the *Plymouth* was remodeled into recitation rooms and quarters.

In August 1860, the historic frigate *Constitution* replaced the *Plymouth* as school ship. It, too, was remodeled into a school and home for more than a hundred midshipmen. Gas and steam for lighting and heating were piped to the *Constitution*, which was approachable only by boat. Isolated from the upper classes, the midshipmen on the school ship were indoctrinated in the ways of naval life under the charge of Lieutenant George Rodgers. "We grew into ship life gradually and naturally," recalled Robley Evans, "and our knowledge of the ship and all her parts was complete."[18] The school ship system helped defuse remaining opposition to the Naval Academy. "In my judgement," wrote Old Navy Captain Samuel F. Du Pont, "the Practice Ship now connected with the Academy . . . induce[s] me to believe that the present system of naval education is very comprehensive and thorough."[19]

The 1860 Board of Visitors agreed. After praising the learning and discipline of the midshipmen, the Visitors lauded the school and the staff:

> [We] desire to record [our] high appreciation of the services of the Superintendent and his subordinates. The institution has prospered in their hands, and promises to the navy a high standard of general and professional knowledge.[20]

The Civil War

The war that superstitious people felt had been presaged three years earlier by the appearance of Haley's Comet settled over Annapolis by degrees. At first there was calm. In accordance with custom, the new fourth class had been administered the oath of loyalty to the Constitution upon the beginning of classes in the fall of 1860. Even after Lincoln's election Academy life showed few outward signs of strain. "Elegant" naval balls and informal hops on board the school ship *Constitution* brought gaiety to the foreboding winter of 1860–61. The Naval Academy Band, prompted by unseasonably good weather, gave a rare February concert, and on 19 March the duty officer's log records that a "Mr. J.L. Lovell (Photographist) came into the Yard and commenced preparations for taking the picture of the graduating class."[21] All of this during the same time in which seven southern states had seceded from the Union.

[18]Evans, pp. 38–39.
[19]Ford Manuscript, Ch. 15, p. 28.
[20]Marshall, *History of the United States Naval Academy*, p. 39.
[21]*Journal of the Officer of the Day*, 19 March 1861.

EPILOGUE

In October 1865 the Naval Academy returned to its former home on the Severn which showed the wear of four years of army use. The superintendent's quarters had become a billiard hall; the Chapel, Lyceum, and library were filthy barracks; horses had chewed back the willow trees; and the encampment of thousands of soldiers had torn up the grounds. Thousands of dollars were needed for restoration. Even Annapolis had "lost its nautical character."[1]

Neither had the Academy prospered in Newport as the near absence of officer instructors, constant detachment of upperclassmen, and large plebe classes resulted in declining academic standards, the outbreak of hazing, and low morale. Boxes of books brought from Annapolis had not even been unpacked. By war's end, the school was near collapse.

And yet, the Civil War was the Old Naval Academy's finest hour. Whereas opponents of the school had feared it would produce effeminate officers, the Academy's antebellum graduates proved themselves worthy descendants of Jones and Decatur in scores of battles. Physical courage was still a hallmark of the American naval officer. The Academy had proved

[1]P. H. Magruder, "The U.S. Naval Academy and Annapolis during the Civil War," *U.S. Naval Institute Proceedings* 72 (April 1946): 71.

Union soldiers treated at the army hospital that was set up on the Academy's grounds during the Civil War. Courtesy: U.S. Naval Academy Special Collections, Nimitz Library

itself in other ways, too. "It was owing to the practical teaching of the Naval Academy," wrote David Dixon Porter, "that we were able during the late war to rapidly build up so large a Navy, and in a short time drill the hardy officers of the mercantile marine into good practical naval officers."[2]

Of the 343 living graduates of the Academy at the outbreak of the war, 174 remained loyal to the Union while 72 chose the Confederacy. The fate of the remainder is unknown. By the end of the war, graduates serving for the North numbered 400, for the South 94.[3] Twenty-three graduates were killed, as were two members of the original 1845 staff. James Harmon Ward was killed by a sharpshooter near the Potomac on 27 June 1861. He was the first Union naval officer killed in the war. Six months later Samuel L. Marcy was killed aboard the USS *Vincennes* in the Gulf of Mexico by a gun that had broken loose during the shelling of a blockade runner.

Other Academy officers met a better fate. Henry H. Lockwood got a colonel's commission with the First Delaware Infantry and, as a brigadier general, led a brigade at the Battle of Gettysburg. Louis M. Goldsborough commanded the Atlantic Blockading Squadron and led a successful attack on Roanoke where he destroyed several Confederate ships. George Blake requested sea duty but was turned down by Secretary Welles who desired that he continue as superintendent.

Another former superintendent whose request was refused by Welles was Franklin Buchanan. Having resigned his commission before Maryland voted on secession, Buchanan tried to withdraw it when it became apparent that Maryland would stick with the Union. Secretary Welles disallowed the withdrawal and Buchanan signed on with the South. He commanded the ironclad *Merrimac* when it wreaked havoc on Union blockaders at the Battle of Hampton Roads in March 1862 and then the ironclad *Tennessee* in its desperate but futile defense of Mobile Bay in 1864. Imprisoned for several months following Mobile Bay, Buchanan entered the teaching profession after the war and served as the president of the Maryland Agricultural College (now the University of Maryland) for the 1868–69 academic year. He died in 1874.[4]

While the Civil War had proven the worth of the Old Naval Academy, its graduates proved their worth far beyond 1865. Peter Karsten is correct

---

[2]Ford Manuscript, Ch. 29, p. 19.

[3]Sweetman, *The U.S. Naval Academy*, pp. 74–75. Thomas G. Ford claims that almost all of the southern graduates of Yale, Harvard, Columbia, and Princeton, and about half of those at West Point, "espoused the rebel cause."

[4]George Dewey wrote of Franklin Buchanan: "It is one of the anomalies of history that one who had such strict loyalty to States' as opposed to national rights should have been the most conspicuous organizer of that school whose graduates, in the Spanish War, struck the blows which did so much to unite the North and South in a new feeling of national unity before the world." Dewey, *Autobiography*, p. 11.

in labeling the 1845–1925 period as the Golden Age of Annapolis, for during that period the Academy was the near-sole supplier of officers to the fleet. Considering that its graduates oversaw the expansion of a navy that in 1845 was second to most to one that in 1918 was second to none, the Academy had not done its job badly. No other group of officers was more important to this growth than those schooled at the Old Naval Academy. The same men who had seemed bent on tearing down their school as midshipmen had harnessed their energies for more constructive purposes as adults.

One result of this naval resurgence was the rebuilding of the Naval Academy, accomplished between 1899 and 1913 at the cost of $8,465,000. Fort Severn and the other buildings of the Old Naval Academy were torn down so that only the pair of brick guardhouses at Gate 3 and the naval monuments—Herndon, Mexican and Tripolitan—remained from the antebellum era. The buildings and grounds of the new Naval Academy had some familiar old names: Bancroft Hall, Mahan Hall, Luce Hall, Sampson Hall, Maury Hall, Chauvenet Walk, Stribling Walk, Goldsborough Walk, Buchanan Road, and Blake Road. After fifty years, the Academy was building a tradition.

Its graduates had already taken steps to preserve tradition with the formation in 1886 of the U.S. Naval Academy Graduates' Association,

> established for the purpose of promoting kindly feeling and social intercourse among its members, of fostering the memories of the Naval Academy, and of preserving the records of all the graduates.[5]

The association's founder and first president was none other than Edward Simpson.

Simpson was one of the Date of 1840 midshipmen who had staged the "Lady of Lyons" with which this study began and with which it shall end. Three of the actors met early deaths before the Civil War. In 1862, Midshipman J.B. Smith was killed aboard the *Congress* at the hands of the ironclad *Merrimac* commanded by Franklin Buchanan. Midshipman L. Paulding died a commander in 1867, William N. Jeffers a commodore in 1883. Edward Simpson died in 1888 having obtained the rank of rear admiral. Spirits Club Grand Master, Academy instructor, writer, Civil War hero, Graduates' Association founder, and admiral, Edward Simpson's career typified that of many officers whose years on the Severn were but rehearsal for greater dramas in later life. For the midshipmen who were part of the life and times of the Old Naval Academy, the world was now their stage.

⁵U.S. Naval Academy Graduates Association, p. 4.

Edward Simpson, shown here as a lieutenant commander. A leader for all occasions, the exploits of Simpson and his Spirits Club have become part of Naval Academy legend. Courtesy: U.S. Naval Academy Archives

BIBLIOGRAPHY

A. Reference Works

Albion, Robert Greenhalgh. *Naval and Maritime History: An Annotated Bibliography.* 4th ed. Mystic, CT: Marine Historical Association, Inc., 1972.

Allard, Dean C., and Betty Bern. *U.S. Naval History Sources in the Washington Area and Suggested Research Topics.* 3rd ed. Washington, D.C.: U.S. Government Printing Office, 1970.

Hamer, Philip M., ed. *A Guide to Archives and Manuscripts in the United States.* New Haven: Yale University Press, 1961.

Lewis, Charles Lee. *Books of the Sea: An Introduction to Nautical Literature.* Annapolis: U.S. Naval Institute, 1943.

Masterson, James R., comp. *National Archives: Preliminary Checklist of the Naval Records Collection of the Office of Naval Records and Library, 1775–1910.* Washington, D.C.: 1945.

Navy Department, Naval History Division. *U.S. Naval History: A Bibliography.* 5th ed. Washington, D.C.: U.S. Government Printing Office, 1969.

Phillips, Geraldine N., and Aloha South, comp. *Records of the United States Naval Academy: Inventory of Record Group 405.* Washington, D.C.: National Archives and Records Service, 1975.

Smith, Myron J., Jr. *The American Navy 1789–1860: A Bibliography.* Metuchen, N.J.: The Scarecrow Press, Inc., 1974.

U.S. National Archives and Records Service, General Services Administration. *Guide to the National Archives of the United States.* Washington, D.C.: 1974.

B. Sources

1. ARCHIVAL RECORDS

Annapolis, Md. Naval Academy Archives. *Catalogue of the Library of the U.S. Naval Academy, Annapolis, Md., 30 June 1860.*

Annapolis, Md. Naval Academy Archives. *Journal of the Officer of the Day, 1851–61.*

Washington, D.C. National Archives. Naval Records Division. Record Group 405. "Records of the Naval Academy."

Washington, D.C. National Archives. Naval Records Division. Record Group 45. "Records of Naval Shore Establishments."

2. PAPERS, AUTOBIOGRAPHIES, RECOLLECTIONS, CORRESPONDENCE

Allen, Gardner W., ed. *The Papers of Francis Gregory Dallas, United States Navy.* New York: DeVinne Press, 1917.

Ammen, Daniel. *The Old Navy and the New.* Philadelphia: J.B. Lippincott Co., 1891.

Dewey, George. *Autobiography of George Dewey.* New York: Charles Scribner's Sons, 1913.

Evans, Robley D. *A Sailor's Log: Recollections of a Naval Life.* New York: D. Appleton, 1901.

Franklin, Samuel R. *Memories of a Rear Admiral: Who Has Served For More Than Half a Century in the Navy of the United States.* New York: Harper and Brothers Publishers, 1898.

Goodrich, Caspar. "Memorabilia of the Old Navy." *U.S. Naval Institute Proceedings* 30 (December 1904): 823–30.

Mahan, Alfred Thayer. "Old Times at the Naval Academy." *Harper's Monthly Magazine* 115 (June–December 1907): 372–78.

Sands, Benjamin Franklin. *From Reefer to Rear Admiral.* New York: Franklin A. Stokes, Co., 1899.

Seager, Robert, and Doris D. Maguire, eds. *Letters and Papers of Alfred Thayer Mahan.* vol. 1: 1847–1889. Annapolis: Naval Institute Press, 1975.

Selfridge, Thomas O. *Thomas O. Selfridge, Jr., Rear Admiral U.S.N.* New York: G. P. Putnam's Sons, 1924.

3. UNPUBLISHED DISSERTATIONS, MANUSCRIPTS, PAPERS.

Burr, Henry L. "Education in the Early Navy." Ph.D. diss.,Temple University, 1939.

Ford, Thomas G. "History of the Naval Academy." 1887 unpublished manuscript in the Special Collections Division of the U.S. Naval Academy Library.

Glasow, Richard D. "The Establishment of the U.S. Naval Academy and the Beginnings of Formal Technical Education in the U.S. Navy." A paper delivered at the Third Naval History Symposium, U.S. Naval Academy, October 1977.

Lebby, David Edwin. "Professional Socialization of the Naval Officer: The Effect of Plebe Year at the U.S. Naval Academy." Ph.D. diss., Columbia University, 1968.

4. BOOKS, ARTICLES, AND MISCELLANEOUS

Aamold, Walter. "Naval Academy Athletics—1845–1945." *U.S. Naval Institute Proceedings* 72 (April 1946): 105–17.

INDEX

Academic Board: as envisioned by 1845 Board of Examiners, 17; and first academic program, 29–32; as faculty voice, 32; problems during Mexican War, 47; 1848 plan for reform, 66; 1849 reform effort, 67; and 1850 reorganization, 68; 1851 conflict with Navy Department, 76; and 1851 reorganization, 77, 78; 1852 resolution, 81; on "oldsters," 86; 1853 attempt to keep Stribling, 97; on tobacco use, 109; on educational philosophy, 115; and 1854 graduation certificate, 131; and entrance exams, 137; on school's purpose, 149; make-up under Blake, 186

Academic program: as recommended by 1845 Board of Examiners, 17; in 1845, 29; first textbooks, 30–31; educational philosophy, 31, 51; practical emphasis, 31–32, 81, 186; compared with other colleges, 32; compared with West Point, 32; line officer influence on, 32; after 1850 reorganization, 68; academic departments during 1850s, 80; merit rolls, 82–83, 80–85, *passim*; "too much science," 115; under Goldsborough, 115–17; midshipmen failure rates, 117; and moral education, 149; assessments of, 150; impact on mid-

shipmen, 151; as affected by the Civil War, 197

American colleges: collegiate way, 160; curriculum, 160; elitism, 161, 162; Harvard, 161; Indiana College, 161; Princeton, 161; social origins of students, 161; Transylvania College, 161; University of Michigan, 161; 159–63, *passim*

Ames, Midshipman, 148

Ammen, Daniel, 6

Annapolis, town of: mentioned as site for Naval Academy, 11, 16, 17; history of, 22–23; Harry Matthews's tavern, 37; economy and Naval Academy, 128, 130; antebellum society and culture, 138–41; social relations with Naval Academy, 138–39; as gateway to Washington, D.C., 140; and the Civil War, 182, 197

Apprentice system, 9

Armstrong, Midshipman: intoxicated, 56–57

Authoritarianism, 156

Bancroft, George: biographical sketch, 14; and founding of Naval Academy, 16–18; later life, 44; role in establishing library, 120; Bancroft hall, 200

Band: origins, 96; February 1861 concert, 188
Band of brothers, 154
Barnes, John S., Midshipman, 112, 130
Barron, James, Commodore, 5
Bartow, Theodore, Chaplain, 144
Benjamin, Park: and Naval Academy coat of arms, 99n; on academics and drinking, 115; on hazing, 153; on cruise food, 173
Blacks: employment of, 33, 33n, 34, 126; in Annapolis, 93; abused, 153, 155, 156; attitude toward, 156n
Blake, George S., Captain: mentioned, 122, 176; wife's role, 140; biographical sketch, 182, 184; and midshipmen discipline, 184–85; relations with professors, 186; and move to Newport, 192–93, 195; during the Civil War, 199; Blake Road, 200
Blake, Midshipman: intoxicated, 39
Board of Examiners: and founding of the Naval Academy, 17; function and influence, 32; questions in 1846, 41; their wives, 42; 1846 report, 44; 1848 report, 65; 1852 report, 84–85; on "oldsters," 86; endorses building plan, 91; and guard house, 91; and 1851 land purchase, 93; recommends a band, 96; and 1854 graduation, 130
Board of Visitors: function, 32; and 1850 reorganization, 70; 1853 report, 98; 1857 report, 98; relation to Board of Examiners, 98n; and steam training, 119; and 1859 library restrictions, 122; recommendations on officer instructors, 123; 1859 report, 185; 1860 report, 188
Bowen, Midshipman: intoxicated, 178
Brintnall, Midshipman: disrespectful, 107
Buchanan, Franklin, Commander: selected as first superintendent, 18; biographical sketch, 19, 21–22; as a disciplinarian, 21, 22, 28, 38–39; sensitive side, 22n; opening remarks, 27–28; educational philosophy, 31; praised by 1846 Examiners, 44; leaves Naval School, 45; in the Mexican War, 45; on courtmartial board,

61; on 1849 Board of Examiners, 67, 68; and 1851 reorganization, 78; and 1855 Naval Efficiency Act, 131; establishes social relations with Annapolis, 139; on educational standards, 149; and practice ship, 167; during and after Civil War, 199, 199n; Buchanan Road, 200; mentioned, 141, 148
Buchanan, James, President, 184
Budget: for 1855–56, 124–25
Buildings and grounds: in 1845, 24, 26; midshipmen quarters, 32; in 1847, 51; 1847 land purchase, 70; expansion under Stribling, 91–93; expenditures for in 1854–55, 124; expansion under Goldsborough, 125; impact of Civil War on, 197; in early 1900s, 200
Bunce, Midshipman: intoxicated, 111
Bureau of Ordnance and Hydrography, 68, 113
Bureau system, 10
Butler, Benjamin F., General, 192, 193

Cain, John, Midshipman, 130
Calvert, James, Rear Admiral, 163
Campbell, Midshipman, 107
Card pledges, 185, 185n
Chapel: and 1854 graduation, 130, 144; as heart of the service, 148; mentioned, 93, 124
Chaplains: in the Old Navy, 142, 144, 146; and "higher interests," 158
Chauvenet, William A., Professor: biographical sketch, 12; at the Naval Asylum School, 14; attempts to found a naval academy, 14; on first faculty, 18; and 1851 reorganization, 77–79 *passim*; as head of Department of Astronomy, 80; influence on Academic Board, 123; assessment of, 123n; and summer cruise, 167; departure and later life, 186; Chauvenet Walk, 200; mentioned, 122
Chesapeake–Leopard Affair, 23n–24n
Civil War: and professional socialization, 155; coming of, 47, 73–74, 101, 180–82; effect on Annapolis, 182; effect on Naval Academy, 188–99 *passim*

Class system, 78
Clubs: Ballsegurs, 37, 38; Spirits, 37, 38; during Upshur's tenure, 54, 55; and 1850 reorganization, 69. *See also* Lawrence Literary Society
Coffin, J.H.C., Professor, 80, 111
Colton, Walter, Chaplain, 144
Compromise of 1850, 73–74
Congress: funding for Naval School, 34, 91, 124; and midshipmen appointments, 93, 95, 135, 136; and West Point appointments, 162; and Naval Efficiency Act of 1855, 131
Constitution, USS: as school ship, 188; at outbreak of Civil War, 192, 193, 195
Courtmartial, 61
Coventry, 65, 65n, 153
Craven, Thomas T., Lieutenant: entertains midshipmen, 140; as commander of summer cruises, 167–77 *passim*; mentioned, 84
Crossman, Midshipman: intoxicated, 112
Cruise. *See* Summer cruise
Cushman, Midshipman: insubordination, 111

Dahlgren, John A., Lieutenant, 6, 9, 84
Dancing, 139
Dartmouth College case, 160
Davidson, W.F., Passed Midshipman, 99
Decatur, Stephen, 5, 6, 19
Demerits, 69, 87, 87n, 107, 108, 126
Dewey, George, Midshipman: on tobacco use, 108, 109; misconduct at mess, 126; on midshipmen appointments, 135; on Mrs. Blake, 140; on hazing, 152; on nationalism, 158; on Franklin Buchanan, 199n; mentioned, 3, 95, 132
Discipline: drinking problem, 1, 37–39, 54–57, 66–67, 88–91, 105–06, 111–12, 178, 184–85; in general, 3, 48, 86–91, 106, 185; among Old Navy midshipmen, 6, 8; at the Naval Asylum School, 12; and the *Somers* Mutiny, 16; Buchanan's philosophy of, 21, 27–28; first regulations, 28–

29; in Buchanan's first quarterly report, 35; and midshipmen clubs, 37–38; vandalism, 38, 57, 67, 185; AWOL, 38, 54–55, 57, 66; dismissals, 38, 61, 65, 90, 106, 110; reprimands, 39; suspensions, 39, 57, 90, 106, 107, 111, 112; tobacco use, 39, 55, 108–09, 185; pranks, 42, 52, 52n, 53, 67, 87, 88, 185; Upshur's philosophy of, 48–50; Date of 1841 midshipmen, 52–53; disrespect and insubordination, 56, 106, 107, 109–11; "larder larceny," 56; the Lockwood incident, 56–61; fighting, 67, 106, 185; and 1850 reorganization, 69; under Stribling, 86–91; conduct list, 87n; Goldsborough's philosophy of, 105; swearing, 106; 1854 regulations, 108; new power for superintendent, 114; new regulations in 1858, 184. *See also* Duelling
Dobbins, James C., Secretary of the Navy, 85, 105–07, 111, 114, 126
Dormitories: in 1845, 32–33; under Stribling, 93; under Goldsborough, 125–26; servants for midshipmen, 126
Drinking. *See* Discipline
Duelling: and Naval School regulations, 28; during Buchanan's tenure, 38; in the Old Navy, 62; between Midshipmen Queen and Stevenson, 62, 64; Upshur's attitude toward, 64; between Midshipmen Dallas and Gale, 64–65; threatened, 67
DuPont, Samuel F., Captain, 5, 188

Educational philosophy. *See* Academic program
Eliot, Charles, 161
Elitism: at other American colleges, 161, 162; at West Point, 162
Elliot, Jesse, Captain, 5
Entrance exams: in 1845, 35; after 1850 reorganization, 68
Erben, Midshipman: intoxicated, 106–07
Evans, Robley: on social origins of midshipmen, 136; on life aboard school ship, 188

Examinations: in 1846, 39. *See also* Academic program; Board of Examiners

Executive Department: as police force, 110

Farragut, David Glasgow, Commander, 6, 61

Fencing, 80, 84

Fillmore, Millard, President, 88, 141

Flogging, 10

Flusser, Charles W., Midshipman: on secession, 191, 191n

Foote, Henry D., Midshipman: tarred and feathered, 153

Ford, Thomas G.: on quality of graduates, 85; on midshipmen appointments, 95, 135; and library, 121–22, 122n; on the purpose of education, 149; assessment of academic program, 150; exhibiting racism, 156; on war, 157; on summer cruise, 167; and 1859 discipline, 185; on sectionalism, 191n; mentioned, 137, 159, 192n, 195, 199n

Fort Adams, 194, 195

Fort Severn: transfer to navy, 16, 18; history of, 23; and American defensive strategy, 24; description in 1845, 24, 26; mentioned, 200

Founding: early attempts, 11–12; spurred by new technology, 12; and officers' attitude, 12; Chauvenet's attempt, 14

Franklin, Samuel R., Rear Admiral, 8

Funding, 34, 91, 124

Garland, Midshipman: intoxicated, 106

Girault, Arsene, Professor: biographical sketch, 42; and 1846 exams, 42; founds church in Annapolis, 138; mentioned, 122

Goldsborough, Louis M., Commander: biographical sketch, 103; relations with Academic Board, 105; philosophy of discipline, 105; disciplinary problems, 106–14 *passim*; and 1854 graduation, 130; and jobbery, 130; scientific curriculum, 150; during the Civil War, 199; Goldsborough Walk, 200; mentioned, 98, 124

Goodrich, Caspar, 154

Grades: on daily recitations, 30; computation of, 31; in 1846, 40; and 1850 reorganization, 68

Graduation: first, in 1854, 130; certificate of, 130–31

Graham, Secretary of the Navy, 126

Grant, Ulysses S., President, 109

Green, Joseph F., Commander, 175

Gunnery, 84, 170

Hanged in effigy: Lockwood, 60; Scott, 112

Harvard, 80, 85

Hazing: and professional socialization, 152; according to Dewey, 152; according to Mahan, 153; during the Civil War, 197

Henshaw, Secretary of the Navy, 14

Herndon Monument, 141, 142, 200

Holliday, James, 155

Honor: and duelling, 62

Hopkins, William F., Professor: biographical sketch, 80; requests pay increase, 123

Huntington, Samuel; on social origins of naval officers, 134; on militarism, 157

Ideals: Annapolis ideal, 133, 134, 162; and religion, 146, 147; moral education, 148; according to Karsten, 155; authoritarianism, 156; racism, 156n; nationalism, 158; gentleman ideal, 192

Janowitz, Morris, 149, 151, 155, 157

Jeffers, William N., Midshipman, 99, 157

Jones, George, Chaplain: at 1846 exams, 41; biographical sketch, 141; as curator of Lyceum, 141; sermons, 147; advocate of summer cruise, 167; mentioned, 144, 146

Jones, John Paul, 87n, 133, 134, 159

Jones, William, Secretary of the Navy, 11

Karsten, Peter; thesis, 134–63 *passim*

Kearney, Midshipman: fighting, 112

Kennedy, John P., Secretary of the Navy, 89, 90, 96, 97

King, Darius, 33–34, 126
King, Ernest, 95

Lady of Lyons, 1, 3, 200
Lawrence, James, Captain, 3
Lawrence Literary Society, 122, 144
Lebby, Edward: professional socialization, 152, 154, 155
Liberty, 69, 91n
Library: beginnings, 31; midshipmen use of, 120–22
Lincoln, Abraham, President, 188, 192
Line–staff controversy, 119
Livingston, Midshipman: disrespectful, 106
Lockwood, Henry H., Professor: at Naval Asylum School, 14; study of West Point, 17; on first faculty, 18; biographical sketch, 57, 59; as infantry drill instructor, 59, 60, 70, 193n; hanged in effigy, 60; role in 1851 reorganization, 77–78; and gunnery, 84, 119–20; requests pay increase, 123; and midshipmen mess, 126; on first summer cruise, 167; during the Civil War, 199; mentioned, 122, 144, 156
Luce, Stephen B., Midshipman, 3, 52, 200
Lyceum, 141

McDonough, Thomas, 5
McGary, Midshipman: racism, 155
McGiffin, Philo, Midshipman, 57n, 59n
McThorne, Henry, Midshipman: intoxicated, 105–06, 157
Mahan, Alfred Thayer, Midshipman: on officer-midshipmen relations, 110–11; on uniform regulations, 128n; and midshipmen social life, 140; criticizes sermons, 147–48; on hazing, 153; placed in Coventry, 153; relations with classmates, 154; on authoritarianism, 156; on black cadet at West Point, 156n; on war, 157; and navalism, 159; and cruise life, 174; on sectionalism, 190; Mahan Hall, 200; mentioned, 3, 99, 132
Marcy, Samuel, Passed Midshipman: at the Naval Asylum School, 14; role in transfer of Fort Severn, 16; study of West Point, 17; appointed to first

faculty, 18; on 1850s faculty, 122; on first summer cruise, 167, 169; killed in the Civil War, 199
Mason, John Y., Secretary of the Navy, 14, 34
Matthews, Edmund O., Rear Admiral, 93
Maury, Matthew Fontaine: appointed a midshipman, 6; reformer, 9, 10; and summer cruise, 167; Maury Hall, 200
Maxwell, Midshipman: intoxicated, 106
Mayo, W. K., Acting Master: choked by midshipman, 109–11
Merit rolls, 115
Merrimac, USS, 132, 141, 199
Messhall: under Darius King, 33–34; bill of fare, 126–28
Mexican Monument, 45, 141, 200
Mexican War: outbreak, 44–45; impact on Naval School, 45, 47–48
Midshipman organization: and 1850 reorganization, 70; under Blake, 185
Midshipmen appointments: in the Old Navy, 5–6; entrance requirements, 31, 35, 136; after 1851 reorganization, 78–79; by Congress, 93; and politics, 95, 135; compared with 1930s, 135n; geographic distribution, 136
Miles, Alfred, Midshipman, 134
Militarism, 138n, 157, 158
Miller, Joseph N., Midshipman, 130
Mish, Midshipman: misconduct in chapel, 148
Mitchell, Charles, Midshipman: AWOL and intoxicated, 57
Monroe, Midshipman: disrespectful, 56
Morris, Charles, Commodore, 96, 98, 113, 114

Nationalism, 158
Naval Asylum School: establishment of, 12; course of instruction, 14
Naval Efficiency Act of 1855, 10, 131, 131n
Naval Lyceum, 9
Naval Magazine, 144
Naval officers: relations with midshipmen, 110–11; definition of, 133; social origins, 134–35; ideals, 135, 155; evaluated as instructors, 186n

Naval School: established, 18; buildings and grounds in 1845, 26; opened by Buchanan, 27–28; funded by Congress, 34
Negroes. *See* Blacks
Newport, Rhode Island, 193, 195
Nimitz, Chester, 95
Nourse, Joseph E., Professor, 147

Observatory, 93, 124
Ogden, Midshipman: intoxicated, 178
O'Kane, Midshipman, 148
Old Navy: description of, 3–8; reform movement, 8–10; end of, 132
Oldsters: described, 35–36; of the 1841 date, 52; disciplinary problems 86–87; mentioned, 87

Pay, 33, 91, 124n
Perry, Matthew C.: as Old Navy reformer, 9; on the 1846 Board of Examiners 41–42; on the 1852 Board of Examiners, 84; on "Star Chamber Board," 131; mentioned, 101, 141
Perry, Oliver Hazard, 5
Pfeiffer, P., Bandmaster, 96
Phoenix, Midshipman: intoxicated, 178
Pierce, Franklin, President, 113, 131, 141
Plymouth, USS, 117, 172, 179, 180
Politics: and midshipmen appointments, 5, 6, 50, 135, 137; and appointments to West Point, 162
Porter, David Dixon, Rear Admiral, 165, 199
Practice ship: recommendations for, 17, 44, 70, 79, 84, 117; school ship under Blake, 186, 188
Preble, USS, 117, 126, 169, 174–77
Professional socialization: and Karsten thesis, 135; defined, 151; affected by military environment, 152; and hazing, 152; and "band of brothers," 154; affected by Civil War, 155
Professional training: in the Old Navy, 8; at the Naval Asylum 14; recommended by 1845 Board of Examiners, 17; in first academic program, 29–32 *passim*; infantry drill, 59–60; under 1850 reorganization, 70; improves under Stribling, 74, 82–85; under Goldsborough, 115–17, 119, 120; school ship, 186, 188

Professors: in the Old Navy, 8; at the Naval Asylum School, 12, 14; role in establishing Naval Academy, 16, 17, 18; on first faculty, 18; on Academic Board, 32; lack of authority, 50; rift with officers, 51; hanged in effigy, 60; made into officers, 61; pay increase, 61; recommendations for reform, 66, 67; rank under 1850 reorganization, 68; influence, 77–78; role in 1851 reorganization, 79; faculty under Stribling, 80; attempt to keep Stribling, 97–98; under Goldsborough, 122–24; civic involvement in Annapolis, 138; at other American colleges, 159–60; at West Point, 162; on first summer cruise, 167; influence wanes under Blake, 186
Puleston, William, 153

Quackenbush, Midshipman: intoxicated, 178

Racism, 155, 156, 156n
Recreation, 91n
Regulations: at the Naval School, 28; on hair and whiskers, 56; after 1850 reorganization, 69; in 1854, 108; on behavior at chapel, 148
Religion, 142–48
Reorganizations: of 1850, 67–71; of 1851, 74, 76–80
Rodgers, Christopher R.P., Lieutenant, 185, 190, 191, 195
Rodgers, George, Lieutenant, 188, 193
Roget, Edward A., Professor, 80
Routine: in 1845, 29, 30
Rudolph, Frederick, 160, 161
Ryland, William, Chaplain, 144

St. Johns College, 139
Sampson, William T., Midshipman, 3, 190, 200
Sands, Benjamin F., 6
Schley, Winfield Scott, 3, 173, 190
Scott, Acting Master, 112, 123
Seager, Edward, 80
Sectionalism, 190
Selfridge, Thomas O., Midshipman: first graduate, 130; and "band of brothers," 154; on nationalism and service loyalty, 159
Sigsbee, Charles, 150

Simmons, Midshipman: fighting, 67
Simpson, Edward, Midshipman: on
midshipmen quarters, 26; and 1846
Naval Ball, 34; as Spirits Club
Grandmaster, 37; suspended, 39;
writes textbook, 99; apprehends in-
toxicated midshipman, 106–07; in-
vestigates midshipmen mess, 127–
28; on dancing, 139; on Academy
education, 154; on nationalism, 158;
recommends chaplains for summer
cruise, 178, 178n; on school ship,
179
Sims, William, 95
Social life, 1, 34, 35n, 138–41, 188,
191
Somers Mutiny, 16, 95, 135
Southard, Samuel L., Secretary of the
Navy, 6, 11
Spence, Midshipman: AWOL, 66
Spencer, Philip, Midshipman, 16, 95,
135
Spirits Club, 99, 122, 139, 200
Steam propulsion: and origins of Naval
Academy, 12; training in, 85, 119,
167
Stewart, Charles S., Chaplain, 142, 144
Stribling, Cornelius K., Commander:
relieves Upshur, 70; biographical
sketch, 74, 76; role in 1851 reorganization, 77, 80; as an administra-
tor, 97; as a disciplinarian, 97; leg-
acy, 97; departure and later years,
98; and Naval Efficiency Act of
1855, 131; report on 1851 summer
cruise, 170; Stribling Walk, 200
Stribling, John M., Midshipman, 130
Summer cruise: and the 1851 reorganization, 78; under Stribling, 84;
under Goldsborough, 117; importance of, 165; departure of in 1860,
165; early advocates of, 167; runs
aground in 1851, 169; midshipmen
performance on, 170, 178–80; at sea
routine, 171; getting underway, 171;
dangers, 172; seasickness, 172; feeding the midshipmen, 172–73; overcrowding, 173; disease, 174; portcalls, 175–77; discipline problems,
178; homecomings, 180
Superintendent. *See* Blake, Buchanan,
Goldsborough, Stribling, Upshur
Swann, Thomas, 76n, 126, 128, 173

Taylor, Midshipman: intoxicated, 111
Thomas, Midshipman: intoxicated, 112
Tillotsen, Midshipman: AWOL, 57; in-
toxicated, 66
Tobacco: pledges not to use, 109, 185;
use by midshipmen, 108–09
Tocqueville, Alexis de, 157
Todd, Henry D., Midshipman, 130
Toon, Midshipman: intoxicated, 106
Toucey, Isaac B., Secretary of the
Navy, 184, 190
Tradition, 141–42, 200
Tripolitan Monument, 142, 200

Uniforms, 29, 69, 69n, 128
Upshur, Abel P., Secretary of the
Navy, 6, 95
Upshur, George P., Commander: biographical sketch, 48; philosophy of
discipline, 48; problems, 50–51; departure and later life, 70; and jobbery, 130; and racism, 155; plea for
practice ship, 167; mentioned, 148
U.S. Naval Institute *Proceedings*, 144

Vagts, Alfred, 157
Van Wyck, Midshipman: fighting, 67

Walker, Midshipman, 110
Ward, James Harmon, Lieutenant: at
Naval Asylum School, 14; on first
faculty, 18; views on academic program, 51, 150; biographical sketch,
52; subject of midshipmen pranks,
52, 54; advice to parents of midshipmen, 152; killed in Civil War, 199
Welles, Gideon, Secretary of the Navy,
192, 193, 195, 199
West Point: as model for Naval
Academy, 17, 27; course of instruction compared with Naval Academy,
80, 81, 85; politicized appointments
process, 95; methods of discipline,
114; hazing at, 153; and elitism,
162
Whitaker, Midshipman: intoxicated,
66, 67
Whitlock, Midshipman: intoxicated, 38
Wilson, Woodrow, President, 159

Yancey, Midshipman, 190n